The Big Book of
100
Little
Activities

The Big Book of
100
Little
Activities

Laura Minter
& Tia Williams

First published 2016 by
Guild of Master Craftsman Publications Ltd
Castle Place, 166 High Street, Lewes,
East Sussex, BN7 1XU

Reprinted 2018, 2020, 2021

Text © Laura Minter and Tia Williams, 2016
Copyright in the Work © GMC Publications Ltd, 2016

ISBN 978 1 78494 245 8

Publisher Jonathan Bailey
Production Jim Bulley
Senior Project Editor Virginia Brehaut
Editor Hazel Songhurst
Managing Art Editor Gilda Pacitti
Designer Ali Walper
Illustrator Mia Underwood

Set in Cabin and Riffic
Colour origination by GMC Reprographics
Printed and bound in China

**For Lilah
and Grayson**

Contents

Playing and performing

Little laboratory

Paint and print

Dressing up

Introduction

Welcome to your go-to boredom-busting manual! We know that entertaining kids isn't easy. They can be fickle, they are soon bored and inspiration for activities can dry up all too fast. With this in mind, we have put together a range of simple projects to fit a multitude of moods, interests and whims – from arts and crafts, to messy makes and simple science experiments, along with activities for rainy days inside and for sunny outdoor play.

WE WROTE THIS BOOK BECAUSE WE NEEDED IT! We have four children between us and we love crafting with them, but we sometimes struggled to find inspiration for things to do with them. We couldn't always think of new ideas that would keep them engaged, which we could adapt to suit their moods, interests and the materials we had to hand. So we created a collection of projects that are simple to follow, clearly illustrated and easy to adapt. Most importantly, they are tried and tested – every one has been made for and with our kids. If something didn't work or didn't go down well, it didn't make it into the book. They're picky little guinea pigs!

We believe that getting crafty with your kids is one of the most important things you can do. It teaches children to express their thoughts and feelings, it helps them to concentrate, to relax and to use their imaginations. It also develops a broad range of motor skills – from learning to control a pen or cut with scissors, to mastering a needle and thread. Plus, turning old containers and cartons into toys they will treasure is a great way to teach children about the value of recycling.

For most of the projects, the materials required can be either found at home, or picked up at your local craft shop. You don't need to buy elaborate materials; crafting can be as inexpensive as you want it to be. For projects that require an unusual item, there is information on where to buy it. Look at the materials section that follows for advice on the basic essentials and on the items to stock up with for the specific projects in this collection.

The activities in this book are aimed at pre-school children, but they may be enjoyed by younger and older ones too. We have tried to show how projects can be adapted to suit different ages wherever possible. Younger children will obviously need more guidance and supervision, whereas older ones can work more independently and should be encouraged to adapt the projects to suit their own style.

Getting started

This section provides an overview of all the basic items you'll need for the activities in this book, along with some tips and safety advice.

Things you'll need

PAINT, BRUSHES AND SPONGES The activities use child-friendly, washable paint unless stated otherwise. It's a good idea to have a range of brushes in different sizes, as well as sponges, combs and other things that allow children to play with the texture of the paint. Keep a stack of paper plates handy to use as paint palettes.

COLOURING PENS, PENCILS AND CRAYONS Wax crayons, pencils and colouring pens are all used in this book. Permanent markers (used under supervision) are also great for adding colour to plastic or rubber.

PAPER AND CARD A mixed pack of coloured paper and card, and a set of paper plates are the starting point for all sorts of projects, from painting, printing and collage to masks, models and musical instruments.

SCISSORS Child-friendly scissors will encourage fine motor development. Some types have blades that give different cutting patterns, such as wavy lines or zigzags.

STICKY TAPE Double-sided tape is a best buy for crafting with kids. Mess-free and with instant stick, it's a total winner! Masking tape, duct tape, conventional clear tape and decorative tapes are also must-haves.

GLUE Glue sticks and PVA glue are essential, as well as strong glue (for adult use only).

ACETATE AND CONTACT PAPER You can use acetate sheets to create a mould for a plaster of Paris project, and contact paper is fantastic for a whole range of activities – it's quick and easy to use and involves no mess.

Don't be daunted if this seems like a lot of materials – you'll probably have most of them already and you can always build up your stock gradually.

FELT AND EMBROIDERY THREAD Felt is a great fabric to have in your stash – it is inexpensive, doesn't fray and comes in a range of bright colours. A mixed pack in a variety of colours is a great resource. Use embroidery thread for hand-sewn projects and finer sewing thread when using a sewing machine. Use a large-eyed embroidery or plastic child-friendly needle.

PIPE CLEANERS Bendy, colourful pipe cleaners are easy for small hands to manipulate and are fantastic for all kinds of self-contained projects. No crafting cupboard is complete without a pack or two!

SHAVING FOAM This is great for crafting and a nice sensory experience for little ones.

EMBELLISHMENTS Googly eyes, buttons, beads, sequins, glitter, pompoms, ribbons and feathers add a fun finishing touch to any project.

Safety

It's really important when crafting with younger kids to make sure they are properly supervised when using equipment. Most of the projects in this book have elements a child can do and elements an adult should do. Items such as craft knives, sharp scissors and strong glue must only be used by an adult. Other materials and processes that should be done by an adult are stated, where applicable, in the projects.

RECYCLABLES Raid the recycling box for cardboard tubes and boxes, plastic containers and glass jars. They can be transformed into all sorts of wonderful things! Keep them in a box if you have the room, so that you can rummage through whenever you feel like making something.

KITCHEN STAPLES Check out your kitchen for useful crafting materials – straws, ice, lollipop sticks, ziplock bags, cocktail sticks, pasta, vegetables, aluminium foil, cling film, salt and food colouring all feature in our activities! A set of plastic bowls, an old tray and a baking sheet are handy, too.

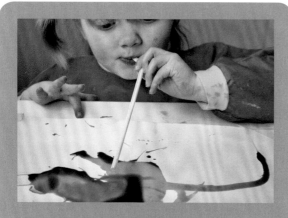

Crafting clothes

Old clothes are perfect for crafting in, so keep hold of any T-shirts that get stained or ripped and pop them with your craft stash. If you don't have to worry about damaging clothes it will make the activity more easy going for everyone. A long-sleeved wipeable apron as a cover-up is a good idea and can be purchased cheaply. Or, you could use an old adult-sized T-shirt on top of the children's clothes. With messy makes, keep sleeves rolled up to avoid them being dragged through paint. Remember to think about your clothes too – even if you're not the one crafting, you may still get covered in paint!

Use an old wipe-clean tablecloth or plastic sheet to cover surfaces and floors when crafting. This makes the clean-up process so much easier. You can even shake the sheet outside when finished to save sweeping up all the mess!

Tips for crafting with kids

BE ORGANIZED AND PREPARED Store things neatly so that you can find what you need at a moment's notice – kids won't always wait patiently while you rummage around for a glue stick!

KIDS HAVE SHORT ATTENTION SPANS Lay everything out in pots within easy reach before starting an activity – and accept that they can be distracted as fast as it takes to boil the kettle!

FIND A PLACE TO STORE ALL YOUR CRAFTY BITS A large box with a lid works well. Keep trinkets like buttons, beads and sequins in old glass jars, stored upside down so that you can easily see what you've got.

BE PREPARED FOR MESS It's all part of the fun and it will all (usually!) wipe away at the end. Think ahead and cover surfaces, use old clothes and have rags nearby for wiping up spills and messes.

LET THE KIDS LEAD THE WAY Kids may well interpret the activity differently to you. Don't expect it to always go in the direction you had imagined. You can steer them a little, but if they take their own path that's great, too. Sitting with them while you make your own version of a project is a good way to show what you were intending, and will stop you wanting to take over.

1 Flower press card

Finding the flowers is all part of the fun for this activity. You can press and transform the prettiest into a card in a few easy steps. Blotting paper will absorb the moisture that comes out of the flowers and prevent colour stains on your favourite books.

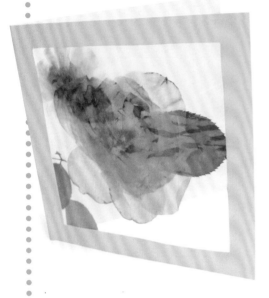

1 Check that the flowerheads and leaves are clean and dry before laying them face up onto the blotting paper. Lay the second sheet on top. Place both in the centre of a large book. Close the book and pile a stack of heavy books on top. Set it aside for a week.

2 Carefully remove the paper sheets from the book and gently peel away each flower.

3 Cut the contact paper to the size you need, peel off the backing and place it sticky side up on your work surface. Arrange the leaves and flowers on the contact paper. The design should be no bigger than the front of your card. Lay another sheet of contact paper on top to seal the flowers. Cut it out a little smaller than the front of your card.

4 On the inside front of the card draw a $^5/_8$in (1.5cm) border and cut it out to create a frame. Finally, use double-sided tape to stick the flower picture inside the frame.

You will need
Fresh flowerheads and leaves
2 sheets of A4 blotting paper
   (absorbent paper)
A few heavy books
Clear contact paper
Blank greetings card
Double-sided tape
Scissors

Nature picture

This activity gives a great opportunity to get outside and see what natural materials you can find to create a piece of art. You could even make a collection of pictures from each season.

You will need
Natural materials, such as leaves, flowers, twigs, feathers
Sheet of cardboard
Doubled-sided tape
Sturdy twig, longer than the width of the cardboard
String
Scissors

1 Take a walk with a container and gather your materials. See if you can also find a twig long enough to make a hanger for your picture.

2 Attach strips of double-sided tape onto the cardboard sheet to form the basic shape of the picture. Peel the backing off the tape and then carefully arrange the materials on top to create a natural masterpiece.

3 Attach strips of double-sided tape onto the back of the picture, at the top. Peel off the backing and position the twig, pressing it down firmly. Cut a length of string and tie it at each end of the twig, ready to hang your picture.

Cookie-cutter bird feeders

Little hands will enjoy getting messy making these tasty treats for garden visitors. You can use any shaped cutter – just avoid ones with narrow indentations, as it can be tricky removing the treats once set.

You will need
Heat-resistant mixing bowl
¼oz (12g) sachet gelatine
3½fl.oz (100ml) boiling water
12oz (350g) wild bird seed
Fork
6 circular cookie cutters,
    at least 1½in (3cm) deep
Baking tray lined with baking
    parchment
Spoon
Scissors
Drinking straw
6ft (2m) twine
Large bead or short length
    of dowel

1 Empty the gelatine sachet into a bowl and add 3½fl.oz (100ml) of boiling water. Mix with a fork until dissolved. Gradually add seed to the liquid and mix, then keep adding seed until all the liquid is absorbed. Once cool, you can mix using your hands. Pick up a handful to check the consistency – it should be firm but moist! If liquid dribbles out then add more seed.

2 Place the cookie cutters onto the lined baking tray. Spoon the mixture inside and press it down until tightly compacted. Cut a 2in (5cm) length of straw and push it into the middle of the mixture. This will make a hole for threading with the twine to hang up the feeder.

3 Leave the feeders in a warm place to harden for a few hours, or overnight. Remove the cutters carefully and ease out the straw. Thread a length of twine through the hole and tie a short length of dowel or a bead onto the end of the thread. Hang the feeders from a suitable branch and wait for the birds to arrive for lunch!

Be patient! Don't expect the birds to come immediately. They may take a day or so before they approach their new cafe.

Peanut butter tube

Make this quick feeder in winter. Simply spread smooth peanut butter onto the outside of a cardboard tube. Sprinkle bird seed onto a tray and roll the tube in the seed until it is covered. Thread twine through the inside of the tube and it's ready to hang.

4 Bug hunt

A bug hunt is a fantastic way to get kids outside learning about nature, and it encourages them not to be scared of the creatures that share our outdoor spaces.

You will need
Open jar or tub
Magnifying glass
Plastic spoon

For a brilliant bug hunt follow these tips:

• Bugs are easy to find, but you'll need to lift rocks, flowerpots or dig a bit of soil up to find them. They like nice warm, sheltered and often damp spots. Search on and under window ledges and in other outdoor corners for spiders. Have a good look at the structure of their webs, too!

• Create a little checklist and tick off the crawlies as you find them.

• Put some grass, soil and leaves at the bottom of your container before adding your bugs. Leave the container open or punch air holes in the lid, so your creatures can breathe.

• For a closer look, gently scoop up bugs using a plastic spoon so that they don't get squished.

• Take paper and pencils, so you can draw pictures of your bugs before you put them back where you found them.

Four fun bug facts

1 Slugs have four noses.

2 Snails can sleep for three years in one go.

3 It takes about one hour for a spider to build a web.

4 Ladybirds can have up to 20 spots (but some have none!)

Fingerprint tree

It's nice to build up this tree painting in three stages: the trunk and branches first, then the leaves, then the fruit. You can talk to children about the seasons as you do each stage.

You will need
Child-friendly paints
Paper
Paintbrush and plate

5

1 Paint the basic brown tree shape (the trunk and branches only) carefully onto the paper.

2 When dry, pour green paint onto your plate, plus a little yellow and white so that you can create a few different shades. Mix the colours using a paintbrush and then dip fingertips into the paint. Press leaves all over the tree and leave it to dry.

3 Finally, dip fingertips into red paint to create some bright, juicy apples.

If you don't have time to wait for the tree to dry before printing the leaves, draw the trunk with colouring pens instead.

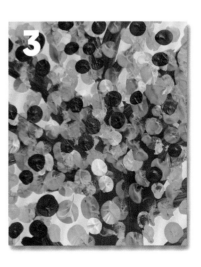

6

Cress heads

Make sure you keep these little cress characters in a sunny spot and add a little more water each day. They will take about a week to get a full head of hair. Then you can then give them a trim and eat the crops.

1 Cut off and discard the lip of the yoghurt pot.

2 Cut a strip of card long enough to wrap around the pot (with a little overlap) and about ¼in (5mm) wider than the height. Add a face using colouring pens.

3 Stick lengths of double-sided tape onto the back of the card, adding extra where it will overlap. Stick the strip around the pot, making sure the pot base and bottom edge of the card line up.

4 Put a couple of balls of cotton wool inside the pot and add enough water to moisten them. Sprinkle on a few cress seeds and add a little more water to dampen them.

You will need (for each cress head)
Small yoghurt pot
Scissors
A4 sheet of coloured card
Colouring pens
Double-sided tape or glue
2–3 cotton wool balls
Cress seeds

Place your cress characters in a sunny spot and watch their hair grow!

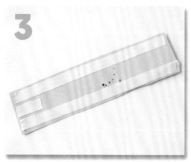

Nature mobile

For this mobile you need items that can be attached easily with twine, so look for twigs, leaves and flowers with long stems.

1 Go on a nature hunt to collect your materials. Bunch leaves and flowers together and tie them with twine. Cut the twine to different lengths so that the bunches will hang at varying heights.

2 Tie twigs together using coloured wool or more twine. Arrange them in overlapping shapes, such as crosses, triangles or squares, and wrap wool around the joins to hold them together. Add a length of twine to each twig for hanging.

3 Fasten your hanging pieces onto the hoop. If you want something to hang from the middle, loop lengths of twine around opposite sides of the hoop and tie them together. Add colour by wrapping yarn around sections of twigs and the hoop.

4 Divide up the bells and thread them onto the ends of two lengths of twine and then tie them onto the hoop.

5 Wind four lengths of twine, tied together at the top, around the embroidery hoop, to make the hanging loop.

You will need
Mixture of leaves, twigs
   and flowers
Scissors
Small ball of twine
Coloured scraps of yarn
5–6 bells
Embroidery hoop

8

Potato porcupine

Plant grass seed into a hollowed-out potato and watch it bloom into a cute porcupine! Make a whole family by choosing different-sized potatoes. Keep your porcupines in a sunny spot, water every day and they should sprout after about a week.

You will need
Large potato
Teaspoon
2 cocktail sticks
Handful of compost
Grass seed
2 googly eyes
Small bead
Double-sided tape
Scissors
Knife

1 Cut your potato in half lengthways with a knife. Dig out the flesh using a teaspoon to create a hollow – the outside should be about ½in (1cm) thick.

2 Cut the cocktail sticks in half using scissors. Push the sharp ends into the bottom of the potato to make four legs.

3 Fill the hollow three-quarters full with compost. Sprinkle on the grass seed and add a little more compost.

4 Attach the googly eyes and a bead nose to the potato using double-sided tape. Give your porcupine a little drink of water and sit it on a windowsill in a sunny spot. Then wait and watch the magic happen.

Peg butterflies

These colourful butterflies are easy to make. Fix them to a wall with sticky tack to create a pretty holder for pictures and other bits and bobs.

You will need (for each butterfly)
Wooden clothes peg
Child-friendly paint and paintbrush
2 small googly eyes
PVA glue
A4 sheet of coloured card
Pencil and scissors
Embellishments such as glitter, sequins, pompoms and gems

1 Paint the peg all over and leave it to dry. Glue the googly eyes near the top of the longer end.

2 Fold the coloured card in half lengthways and place the peg next to the fold. Mark the length of the opening section of the peg onto the card. Starting at the top mark and ending at the lower one, draw a butterfly half onto the card. Cut out and open up the shape.

3 Stick the decorations onto the wings and add glue at the centre. Pinch the peg over the wings and leave your butterfly to dry.

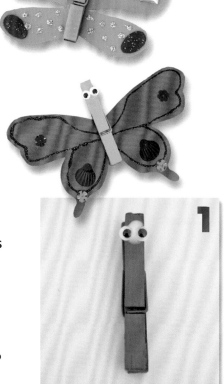

10

Binoculars

These binoculars are a great way to use up items in your recycling box. They can be decorated in any way you like and are perfect for exciting adventures like a bear hunt or looking for buried treasure.

You will need

3 cardboard tubes, 2 x 5in (5 x 13cm)
Child-friendly paints
Paintbrush
Scissors
2 rolls of decorative tape

Strong glue
30in (76cm) length of string
2 split pins
Approx. 30in (76cm) length of ribbon

1 Paint the three cardboard tubes.

2 Once dry, cut one down so that it is 3in (8cm) long. Squash the shorter tube in the middle. Then cover it with decorative tape.

3 Wrap decorative tape around the ends of the tubes.

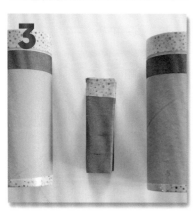

4 To join the binocular pieces together, put strong glue on each side of the squashed tube and stick a long tube either side of it. Tie string around the pieces to hold them in place until the glue has set.

5 To attach the ribbon, push a split pin into the outside of the long tubes. Remove the pin and place the ribbon end over the hole. Push the pin through the ribbon and open the ends inside the tube. Stick tape over the ends to conceal the points.

Messy
makes

11

Squishy sand

This squishy, mouldable sand has a great texture, which is lovely to play with. It should hold its shape like wet sand, making it great for building things with.

Weigh out and pour the sand into the plastic box. Mix the cornflour thoroughly into the sand using your hands. Add the washing-up liquid to the water and stir to combine. Pour in the liquid a little at a time, mixing with your hands until the sand holds together but does not feel sticky.

The sand should hold its shape really well, allowing you to build and shape things easily. Replace the lid when you're done and store the box away till you're ready to play again. Mix in a little more water if the sand dries out.

You will need
10lb (4.5kg) play sand
1 cup cornflour
½ cup water
1 tbsp washing-up liquid
Large, shallow plastic box
   with lid

Sand tools

Spoons, cups and any other interestingly shaped moulds make great additions to your sand tray. Why not add plastic animals and turn it into a zoo with twigs and leaves for trees? Or, try using silicone cupcake cases with pebble toppings for a sand bakery.

Salt painting

Sprinkle salt onto PVA swirls, then let it dry out and drop paint onto the pattern to see the colours bleed into each other. This is a fantastic introduction to colour mixing. For a project like this, which uses only small amounts of paint in lots of colours, an old ice-cube tray makes a perfect paint holder.

12

You will need
Sheet of card
Tray
PVA glue
Container of salt
Watercolour paints and
    paintbrush
Old ice-cube tray or
    small pots
Water

1 Place the card flat on the tray. Pour over the glue, creating patterns and swirls as you do so.

2 Pour salt liberally on top of the wet glue, so that it completely covers the card. Set it aside to dry overnight.

3 Next day, tip away the excess salt.

4 Place a little paint into each section in the ice-cube tray and mix with water to make it runny. Then use your brush to dribble and paint the colours onto the salt.

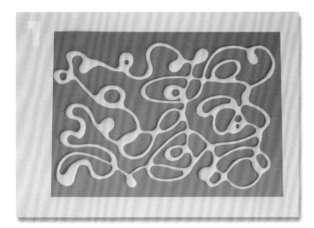

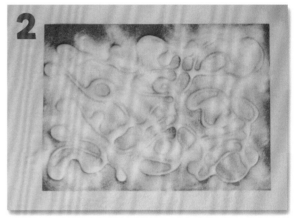

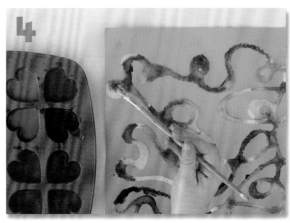

13

Cornflour goop

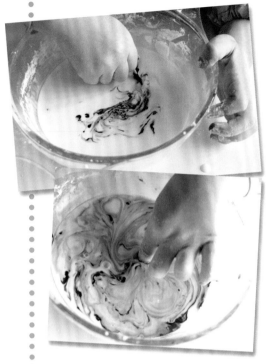

When cornflour and water are combined, something very strange happens: it becomes a liquid and a solid all in one go, or, as Dr Seuss called it, 'Oobleck'. Tap your fingers on it and it feels hard, but leave them there for a second or two and they will sink in and it will feel like liquid. Scoop it up and it cracks like a solid but drips, too.

You will need
Mixing bowl
1½ cups cornflour
1 cup water

Spoon
Selection of liquid food
   colourings

To make it, all you need to do is pour the cornflour into a bowl then add the water a little at a time, stirring until it becomes gooey. When you pull the spoon through the mixture it should crack apart then quickly sink back together and regain its former consistency. Add a few drops of different food colourings – and then play! Mix it around and see how the colours blend, let your fingers sink in and try rolling the oobleck into a ball.

14

Blowing paint

This is a fun way to move paint around a page. Just make sure you practise blowing through the straw first and not sucking the paint up. Yuck!

You will need
Child-friendly paint (thinned with water)
Paper
Straws

Thin the paint with a little water so that it is runny. Put a puddle of it onto the centre of the paper and blow it across the surface through the straw. Make sure you keep the straw quite close to the paint and try blowing it in different directions. If you want to build up layers of paint, make sure each one is dry before adding the next, or you will end up with a brown splodge.

Speedy play dough

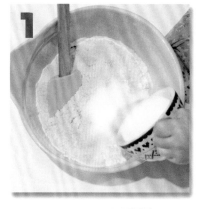

This quick play dough recipe is a great last-minute activity. The dough doesn't need to be heated and stirred so can be ready in ten minutes. Gel food colouring gives brighter colour than liquid and won't compromise the texture.

You will need
2 mixing bowls
Wooden spoon
2 cups plain flour
½ cup salt
1½ tbsp cream of tartar
1 cup boiling water
1 tbsp oil
1 tsp almond or vanilla essence
Gel food colouring in red, blue
   and yellow
Cocktail stick or teaspoon

If you want to make dough in only one colour, add the food colouring to the water before mixing it in.

1 Mix together the dry ingredients in a large bowl. In a separate bowl, mix together the water, oil and essence.

2 Pour the liquid into the dry ingredients and beat with a wooden spoon until combined. Knead into a dough using your hands. If the dough feels sticky add a little flour and if it is cracking add a few drops of water.

3 Separate the dough into three roughly equal pieces. Use a cocktail stick or the end of a teaspoon to drop a little food colouring onto each piece.

4 Fold the colouring into the dough, kneading until it is combined. Add more colouring for a more intense colour.

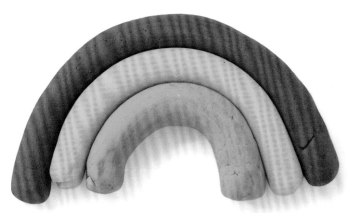

16 Shaving foam marbling

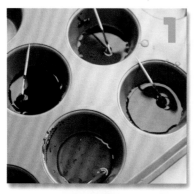

Squirty, messy shaving foam is exciting for children and it has a great texture. Kids will love swirling the colours and making their own card print in this activity. You could also print onto plain brown paper, transforming it into psychedelic gift wrap.

You will need
Muffin tray
Selection of liquid food colourings
Cocktail sticks
Baking tray
Aluminium foil
Shaving foam
Pipette
White card
Ruler
Glitter (optional)

You could add a sprinkle of glitter before the foam dries for some extra sparkle.

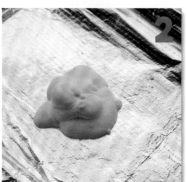

1 Pour a little water followed by a little food colouring into each cup of the muffin tray. Stir with a cocktail stick to combine.

2 Line the baking tray with foil. Spray shaving foam on top and spread it across the tray in an even layer.

3 Use the pipette to drop spots of food colouring onto the shaving foam. Create swirls of colour in the foam using a cocktail stick. Try not to overmix.

4 Place your card on top of the shaving foam and gently pat it down. Starting at one end, carefully peel the card away. Use a ruler to scrape off the excess shaving foam to reveal your marbled print.

17

Shaving foam bath art

This very messy (but contained) activity provides endless entertainment – the whole bathtub becomes your canvas! Buy some cheap shaving foam so you don't feel like you're wasting money.

You will need
Shaving foam
Selection of food colouring
Plastic bowls

Simply squirt shaving foam into plastic bowls and mix food colouring into each one. Then undress your children and pop them into an empty bath. Give them some paintbrushes or just let them mix the 'paint' with their hands and fill the bath with their art. Don't panic about the mess – it all washes quickly away. In fact it actually cleans your bath!

18 Squishy balloon faces

These little fellas feel like friendly stress balls – kids love to squash them into odd shapes and contort their faces. You will need four hands: an adult to hold open the balloon and a child to stuff it with play dough.

You will need
Play dough (about a handful per balloon)
Several balloons
Coloured yarn
Scissors
Coloured permanent markers

1 Roll the play dough into sausage shapes – one per balloon. Push your fingers into the neck of the balloon and pull it open as wide as you can. Kids can then push in the play dough, squashing it inside until the balloon has no more air. Knot the neck of the balloon.

2 For the hair, wrap yarn around your fingers about 10 times. Remove the yarn bundle, tie it in the centre and then onto the neck of the balloon. Snip through the loops.

3 Draw silly faces onto the balloons using permanent markers.

PVA planets

PVA glue is easily coloured and decorated when wet and dries into a translucent, plastic-like material that can be cut into different shapes. It takes a few days to set so do this project in two sessions.

You will need
Child-friendly paints
    in 4 colours
Paintbrush or pencil
4 paint pots
Water
Old plastic tray
PVA glue
Small spoon
Scissors

The PVA glue shouldn't stick to your tray but use an old one just to be on the safe side. You could also use a plate or a lid from an ice-cream tub.

1 Add a dollop of paint to each pot. Mix with a little water until the paint is of a pourable consistency. Pour the glue into a plastic tray, making sure you cover the whole surface. The glue layer should be about ¼in (5mm) thick.

2 Drop spots of paint onto the PVA with a small spoon. Use the end of a paintbrush or pencil to swirl the paint through the glue, being careful not to over-mix the colours. Set the tray aside – and out of reach – on a flat surface for 2–3 days to dry completely.

3 Pull the PVA sheet away from the tray, starting in one corner; you can use a knife to loosen it. Then use scissors to cut out different-sized circles for the planets, including a little Saturn ring from the leftover pieces. Fix your planets onto a window and watch the sun shine through them.

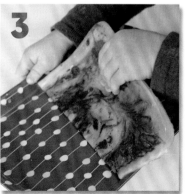

20 Cardboard tube marble drop

This is a really fun indoor activity that can be set up on a large foam board or cardboard sheet for easy storage. You could also tape it to a wall for a more permanent feature. Make the run any size you like – the bigger, the better – or create more than one and have a race!

You will need

Sturdy cardboard tubes
   (5 per run)
A2 foam board or a wall
Scissors
Child-friendly paint
Paintbrush
Decorative duct tape
Marbles or pompoms
Shiny stickers (optional)

1 Arrange the five cardboard tubes on the board to create the run. Play around with the tubes to see which fit together well. For the middle section of the run, cut the tube ends at an angle so they fit neatly. Remember that the tubes need to slant downwards to prevent the marbles getting stuck.

2 Paint the tubes and leave them to dry. If you are having more than one run, choose a different colour for each. Use some decorative duct tape to embellish them.

3 Stick a length of tape inside the top and bottom of each tube. Then, starting at the top of the board, press the tubes into position one by one. Add some large, shiny stickers to the board for extra decoration and you're ready to play!

Arranging your tubes before sticking them down is a good way to get a run that's the right length. Just make sure you number them in pencil once you have the order you want, so there's no confusion when piecing them back together.

On the count of three, simply drop marbles or pompoms down the runs and see whose travel the fastest.

21

DIY den

You will need
Sofa cushions and pillows
2 dining chairs
Blankets, towels and sheets
Heavy books
Clothes pegs

Add mini bunting, battery-operated fairy lights, glow sticks and torches to light up your den.

Building an indoor den is a great way to occupy a rainy afternoon. Here's how to make a fun sofa hideout using materials you'll find around the house.

Start by removing the sofa cushions from the sofa. Prop half of the cushions up against the sofa to form a wall, then prop the rest up opposite them against the back of two dining chairs. Weigh the chairs down with a few heavy books to prevent them from toppling over. Leave a gap for the entrance to the den. Now grab some sheets and blankets and throw them over the sofa, cushions and chairs to create the roof and sides of the den. Tuck them into the sofa and underneath the books to prevent them from falling off. Use clothes pegs to secure the sheets and hold them together. Drape a towel over the entrance to your den for a door and use a clothes peg to keep it closed. Fill your den with sleeping bags, books, comics, games, teddies and of course some hideout-friendly (i.e. not messy!) snacks.

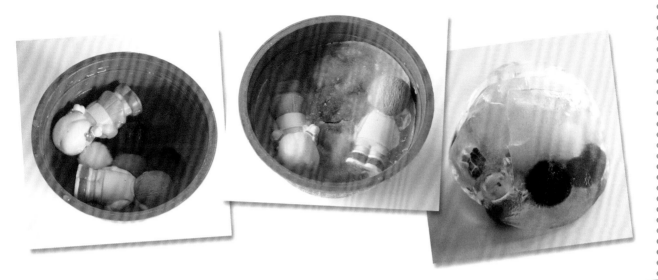

Melting treasure bombs

22

This is a super-simple project – freeze plastic toys in ice to be dug out and discovered by budding excavators. Perfect for a bathtime activity, some rainy-day fun in the kitchen sink, or even outside on a hot day in the paddling pool.

Place the toys into one or more plastic containers (under 4in/10cm is best to avoid boredom and a cold bath!). Fill the containers with water and place in the freezer overnight. Then bring them out at bath time and see how long it takes to free the toys from the ice.

You will need
Selection of small plastic toys
2–3 round plastic containers, 4in (10cm) or less in diameter
Water

If you want to make your melting bombs even more exciting, why not try adding glitter, pompoms or food colouring to the water before freezing?

23 # Guess the flavours game

This is a fun game for a rainy day and a wonderfully sneaky way to get kids to try new foods (shhhh!). Just don't try anything too ambitious, or they'll refuse to taste anything else and the game will be over in a shot.

You will need
Selection of snack foods
4 small bowls
Tray
Clean tea towel
Scarf

Cut up some fruit, crackers and vegetables (plus a sweet surprise, like chocolate buttons) into bite-sized pieces. Divide them into separate bowls, place on a tray and cover with a tea towel so they are hidden. Use a scarf as a blindfold (or ask children to close their eyes) then put a piece of food into their mouth. Young children can shout out their guess or older ones can write down what they think they have just tasted.

Plaster of Paris handprints

24

These 3D handprints are easy to make with plaster of Paris and play dough. You could make other types of prints too – feet, plastic toys or shapes – anything that leaves an imprint in play dough.

1 For the moulds, roll out two circles of play dough, large enough to fit each hand with a little room around the fingers, and at least 1in (2.5cm) thick. Make sure the dough is smooth and level. Place the child's hand onto the dough with the fingers spread out. Gently press the hand into the dough, making sure every part is embedded evenly.

2 Make two acetate ring moulds. For each, cut a strip 6in (15cm) wide and long enough to circle a handprint (you may need to tape two lengths together). Join the strips together using tape. Position each ring over a handprint, then push it firmly down through the play dough. Remove the excess dough around each base and transfer the moulds to a tray.

3 Put the plaster of Paris into a plastic bowl. Stir in the water gently to avoid bubbles. Pour the plaster into the play dough moulds. Tap the moulds lightly to remove air and leave the plaster to set for a few hours.

4 Remove the acetate and peel and rub away the play dough (the dough might be a little soggy now but a little flour will bring it back to life!).

5 Paint the 3D handprints with acrylic paint to make them really pop! Colour each handprint gold and the base white.

You will need
(for each handprint)
Play dough
Rolling pin
Acetate sheet
Scissors
Clear tape
Tray
1 cup plaster of Paris
Plastic bowl
½ cup water
Metal spoon
Gold and white acrylic paint
Paintbrush

! Plaster of Paris heats up as it hardens. An adult should always do the mixing and pouring. Do not put into direct contact with skin.

25 Plaster of Paris pen pots

These pen pots can be made by an adult and then decorated by children. The plaster takes a few days to set so the making and decorating needs to be done in two separate sessions.

You will need (for one pot)
A4 acetate sheet and scissors
Pen and ruler
Cardboard box about
    4in (10cm) in diameter
Masking tape
Short cardboard tube
    (e.g. toilet-roll tube)
Plaster of Paris
A few handfuls of rice
    or lentils
Child-friendly paints
    and paintbrush

!

Plaster of Paris heats up as it hardens. An adult should always do the mixing and pouring. Do not put into direct contact with skin.

1 Make an acetate mould to fit inside the box to stop the plaster from sticking to it. To do this, measure and draw a square slightly smaller than the base of the box. On each side of the square measure and draw a rectangle the same height as the box. Cut out, fold up and tape together making sure there are no gaps. Place this inside the cardboard box.

2 Completely cover one end of the cardboard tube in masking tape. Leaving the other end open, cover the rest of the tube in a smooth layer of masking tape without any gaps. Make up the plaster of Paris following the manufacturer's instructions, mixing enough to fill your mould two-thirds full. Gently pour the plaster into the mould, tapping the sides of the mould lightly to release any air bubbles.

3 Insert the cardboard tube into the centre of the plaster, covered end first. Make sure it is straight and pour the rice or lentils inside to weigh it down. Tape firmly in place and leave it to harden for an hour.

4 Peel away the masking tape holding the cardboard tube. Gently twist the tube and pull it out. Pull the plaster of Paris shape out of the box and cut away the acetate mould. Leave it to dry completely for a day or two. When completely dry, paint and decorate the pots in any style you like.

Masking-tape car track

This car track is a fab way to entertain kids who are stuck indoors. The track can be created together, and doesn't have to be restricted to a small space – it could go up stairways, through furniture tunnels and into other rooms.

You will need
Masking tape
Paper plate
A4 sheet of card
Scissors

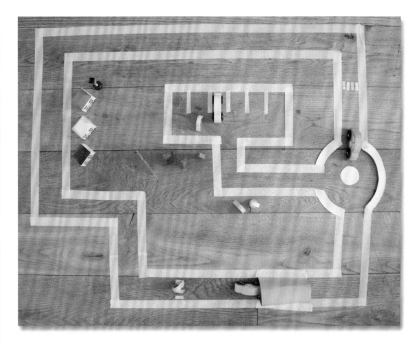

1 Clear a floor space for the start of your track. Use two parallel strips of masking tape to create the road and lay small tape strips across it for zebra crossings. Make a rectangular car park and parking bays.

2 Cut the rim off a paper plate and a small circle out of the centre to create a roundabout. Decide how many junctions you want and snip the number of sections you need from the rim of the plate. Join these to the masking-tape roads and tape the circle in the centre.

3 For a tunnel, bend the card sheet into an arch. Fold up a narrow tab along either side, to make it easy to tape onto the floor. Make sure the tunnel is tall enough for your cars!

27 Alphabet lacing cards

Making up a batch of alphabet lacing cards is a great introduction to sewing and using the letters will also help children to learn their own initials.

You will need
Thick card
Pencil or pen
Scissors
Single hole punch
Shoelace or ribbon
Child-friendly plastic sewing needle

1 The height and width of the letter shape you use should measure approximately 6in (15cm). Draw it onto the card and cut it out. Use the hole punch to make holes all the way round, keeping as close to the edge of the letter as you can.

2 Tie a knot at one end of the shoelace or ribbon to secure it, and thread the other end through the needle. Children can then lace through the letter, stitching round the edge or across the letter.

Ask children to draw their own picture onto cards, for holes to be punched into.

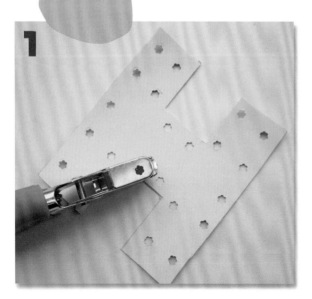

Winter pomander

This will add a festive aroma to your home and is easy to make. You can stick to a traditional orange, or try a lemon or lime for a different look and scent.

You will need
Ribbon
Orange, lemon or lime
Scissors
Pin or sticky tape
Wooden skewer or
    cocktail stick
Jar of whole cloves

1 Cut a length of ribbon long enough to fit around the middle of the orange. Pin or tape it in place.

2 Use the wooden skewer to poke holes all over the orange. Place the holes randomly or in patterns.

3 Push whole cloves into the holes so that they cover the orange completely.

29 Magnetic jigsaw puzzle

Do you have loads of kids' art and not enough wall space? Turning artworks into magnetic jigsaw puzzles keeps them on display and gives children the chance to play with their favourite pictures.

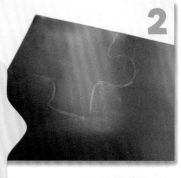

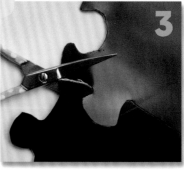

You will need
Artwork printed on photo paper
Pencil and scissors
A4 magnetic sheet
Glue stick
A magnetic surface

> You can stick the picture directly onto the magnetic sheet, but photo paper gives a better finish for the puzzle and you won't need to cut up the original artwork.

1 Choose an artwork that will make a good puzzle, such as one with lots of objects or shapes. Take a photo and scale it to just smaller than A4, then print it onto photo paper.

2 Cut the magnetic sheet to the same size as your printed art. On the magnetic side, draw simple, joined puzzle shapes about 2–3in (5-8cm) square. You can adapt the shapes to make the puzzle easier or trickier if you like.

3 Glue the artwork print onto the non-magnetic side. Wait for the glue to dry and then cut out the puzzle pieces.

4 Pile the pieces onto the fridge or other magnetic surface, then see how quickly your child can fit the puzzle back together!

Alphabet crayons

This is a simple and satisfying way to use up broken crayons. You can create lovely marbled ones by layering up different colours. A silicone mould works best to allow you to ease the crayons out.

Heat the oven to 150°F/70°C/Gas Mark 2. Remove any paper wrappers then chop the crayons into small pieces. Fill the spaces in the moulds with a rainbow mix of colours. Bake in the oven for 8–10 minutes or until all the crayon pieces have melted. Remove from the oven and leave the shapes to cool and harden, then gently pop them out of the moulds.

You will need
Old wax crayons
Knife and chopping board
Silicone alphabet moulds

You can use any mould, but try not to use ones with very narrow parts as the crayons will snap when you take them out.

30

31 Talking frog card

This chatty character is quick and easy to make and perfect for budding puppeteers. The frog's mouth is folded the opposite way to the fold in the card, meaning it can be opened and closed.

You will need
A4 sheets of green and
   red card
Scraps of white card
Pencil and ruler
Eraser
Scissors
Black colouring pen
Glue stick

1 With the green card in landscape format, fold it in half widthways. Measure halfway along the folded edge and draw a 2in (5cm) equal-sided triangle. Draw a line through the centre of the triangle to divide it in two. Cut along this line.

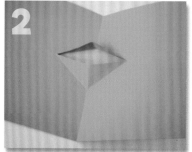

2 Open out the card. Bend up the two triangles, following the pencil lines, at angles to the central fold. When you open and close the card they should move like a beak.

3 Lay the card flat and erase the pencil lines. Draw the outline of half a frog on one side of the central fold. Fold the card in two and cut around the outline.

4 Cut out eyes from white paper and draw on black pupils, then glue in place. Cut a square of red card bigger than the frog's mouth. Glue this carefully onto the back of the card (but don't glue the mouth shut!).

5 Cut a long tongue from the red card and fold it into a concertina. Make a little fly from a card scrap and glue it on the end. Glue the tongue inside the mouth. Now open and close the card to make your frog talk!

Have a go at making other talking animals, such as a duck, dog or penguin. And if you want to turn your chatty creature into a greetings card, simply glue a second card sheet onto the back.

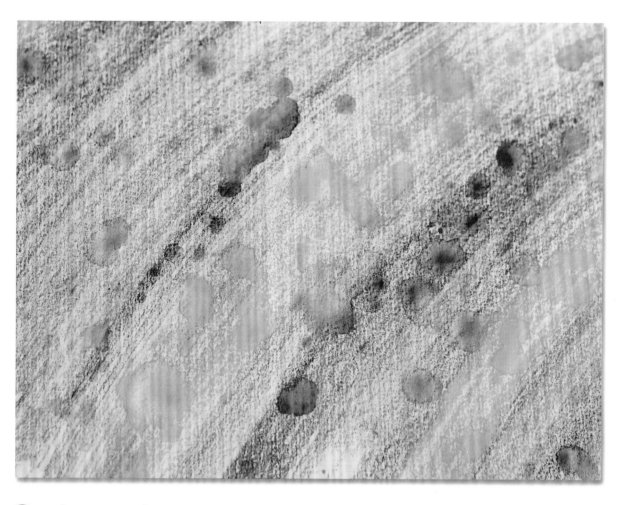

Rain painting

32

Usually when it begins to rain there's a race to get everything inside. With rain painting, it's the opposite! Make sure that you use watercolour pencils for this activity so that the colours will blend together nicely.

You will need
Watercolour pencils
Thick paper
Plastic tray
Rain shower (or bowl of water)

Fill the paper with colourful patterns using watercolour pencils. Place the picture on a plastic tray and leave it outside. Then sit in the window and watch the rain do its work. When the picture is nicely speckled with drops, bring it inside to dry. If it's not raining, create a similar effect by dipping your fingers into a bowl of water and sprinkling it over the paper.

For different effects, try using a pipette or gentle water spray.

33 Pizza faces

These fun pizza faces make a great alternative to boring sandwiches and using bread as a base makes them super simple. Not only a fun cooking activity for kids but also a clever way to get them to eat up their veggies!

You will need
Passata or tomato sauce
Pizza toppings: olives, peppers, tomatoes, sweetcorn, pineapple, ham and pepperoni are all good for faces
Grated mozzarella or cheddar
Sliced bread

Lay out a selection of prepared toppings on the table in easy-to-reach bowls, along with some passata and grated cheese. Spread the passata thinly onto toast, add a sprinkling of cheese then fill the pizza with toppings to create funny faces. Grill until the cheese bubbles, then serve up.

Jam-jar lanterns

These simple lanterns are great fun to make with little ones – they love getting messy with glue and tissue paper! You can make them in different colours and sizes to add a warming glow to a winter's night, or as pretty decorations for a summer party.

You will need
Glass jars in various sizes
Scissors
Tissue paper in 2–3 colours
PVA glue and spreader
Ribbon
Battery-operated tea lights

1 Soak the labels off each jar, remove any grease and dry thoroughly. Cut the tissue paper into approximately 1in (2.5cm) squares.

2 Working in sections, spread a thin layer of glue over the outside of the jar, covering it with overlapping tissue-paper squares as you go.

3 When the outside of the jar is covered, fold and glue a little tissue around the rim to hide it. Spread another thin layer of glue over the tissue paper to seal it and leave the jar to dry for a few hours. Tie a ribbon around the top, pop a battery-operated tea light inside and it's ready to glow.

Paper-weave place mat

Paper weaving is a great way to get little fingers moving. They may find it tricky at first but sitting down next to them and doing your own place mat will really help them to master the art.

You will need
A4 thin card or paper in 4–5 colours
Ruler and pencil
Scissors
Clear tape
Clear contact paper or laminating sheets and a laminator

1 Pick a colour for the base of your weave. With the card or paper in portrait, draw a horizontal line roughly an inch below the top edge. Then draw ten vertical lines at ¾in (2cm) wide intervals, from the horizontal line to the bottom edge. Cut along the vertical lines from the base to the horizontal line.

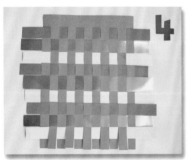

2 Cut up the remaining coloured card sheets into A4 strips approximately ¾in (2cm) wide. They don't all need to be exactly the same width.

3 Take a strip and weave it through the base card. Guide it over the first strip, under the second, over the third, and so on until the end of the row. Push it neatly to the top. Take the next strip and this time guide it under first, then over, then under, and so on. Continue to weave the strips alternately like this until you run out of space.

4 Use scissors to trim the horizontal strips on either side and stick tape along the edges to make a neat seal.

5 Now turn your weave into a place mat by covering the front and back with contact paper, then trim neatly around it. For a thicker, more durable finish you could laminate the mat instead.

35

Felt shape pictures

Using felt scraps to form pictures is a simple way to stimulate the imagination and teach children about basic shapes and patterns. Felt is a great material to use for this because it sticks to itself, so you can make and then remake as many pictures as you like.

You will need
Felt sheets in different colours
Scissors

Set aside one felt sheet for a background and then cut the rest into lots of different-sized geometric shapes. Think about ideas for using the shapes as you cut, to make building the pictures easier.

If kids are unsure what to do with the shapes at first, you can help them by creating your own picture at the same time. They will soon see all the different pictures and patterns they can make.

37

Rain-cloud mobile

Paper-plate mobiles are fun and easy to make. You could also make other weather-themed mobiles to go with your rain cloud. How about a glowing paper-plate sun? Or a colourful rainbow shape?

1 Cut the paper plate in half. Punch two holes in the rim of the curved edge, one either side of the centre, about 4in (10cm) apart.

2 Cover the back of the plate with glue. Tear balls of cotton wool in half and stick them closely together all over the plate. It won't matter if you cover the punched holes. Set the cloud aside to dry.

3 Fold the blue card sheets in half lengthways and cut out lots of different-sized raindrop shapes. You will need about 24 altogether.

4 Cut five lengths of embroidery thread, approx. 18in (45cm) long. Arrange the raindrops on a tray in five vertical lines with four or five droplets to a line. Space the droplets about 3in (8cm) apart. Add a blob of glue to each then lay the embroidery threads on top. Leave about 4in (10cm) clear at the top of each thread. Set the tray aside to let the pieces dry.

5 Arrange the threads on the back of the cloud at different levels so that the drops hang at different heights. Tape in place.

6 Thread about 20in (50cm) of embroidery thread through the holes in the cloud to make a loop. Knot at the back and hang up your mobile.

You will need
A paper plate and scissors
Hole punch
Glue
Cotton wool balls
2 sheets of A4 card, in
    different shades of blue
Tray
Clear tape
Blue embroidery thread
    and needle

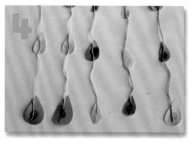

Sticky pictures

Clear contact paper is fantastic for making collage pictures – it's less messy than glue and you don't have to worry about allowing for drying time.

Cut the contact sheet to the size you need, peel off the backing and place it sticky side up on your work surface. Place coloured lollipop sticks round the edge to make a frame then build up your picture. Arrange lollipop sticks around a yellow card circle for a sun, or combine green lollipop sticks with cupcake cases for flowers. Sequins make pretty wings for a butterfly with a lollipop stick body. Fill the sky with pieces of blue tissue paper and add cotton-wool ball clouds.

You will need
Clear contact paper
Coloured lollipop sticks
Coloured card
Coloured tissue paper
Coloured sequins
Cupcake cases
Pompoms
Cotton wool balls

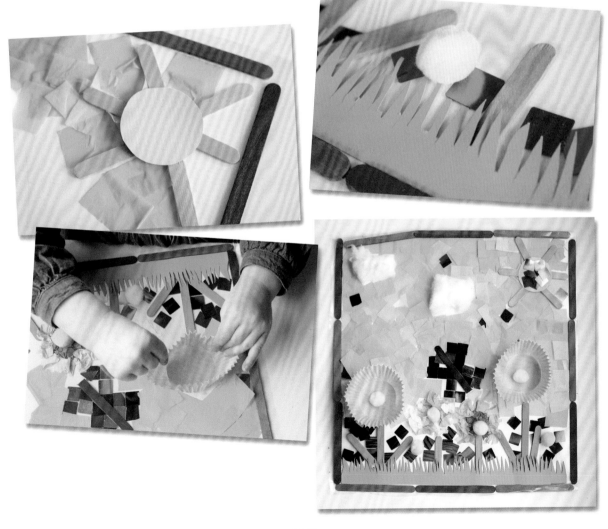

Sunny
day

39

Weather sun catchers

Children will enjoy making and displaying these sun catchers. The light shines through the colourful tissue paper, so they're perfect for sticking on windows.

You will need
A4 card in yellow, blue, white
    and grey
2 plates, about 8in (20cm)
    and 6in (15cm) in diameter
Clear contact paper
Tissue paper in yellow, blue,
    white and grey
Coloured sequins
Pencil and ruler
Scissors
Sticky tack

Little ones can identify what the weather is each day and stick the appropriate symbol onto the window.

1 To make the sun, draw around the larger plate onto the yellow card. Then place the smaller plate inside the circle and draw around this, too. Cut it out using scissors to create a ring and a smaller circle.

2 Cut the smaller circle into eight equal sections to make the sun rays.

3 Cut out a piece of contact paper larger than the ring. Peel off the backing and place it on a surface, sticky side up. Lay the ring onto the contact paper and arrange the rays, making sure they are touching the ring.

4 Cut up yellow tissue paper into small squares. Stick the contact paper and sun onto a window using sticky tack, with the sticky side of the contact paper facing you. Fill the inside of the sun with the tissue paper squares and add a few sequins.

5 Cut a second piece of contact paper roughly the same size as the first. Peel off the backing and gently place it sticky side down over your sun to seal. Smooth out air bubbles and cut away any excess. Use sticky tack or tape to fix the sun catcher to the window.

Making other symbols

You could also make other weather symbols, such as clouds, rain or lightning, in the same way as the sun. Draw cloud shapes onto the white and grey card. Add an inner outline to each shape and use scissors to cut this out. Fill the clouds with white or grey tissue paper and sequins. Add a little yellow lightning bolt and a few rain drops.

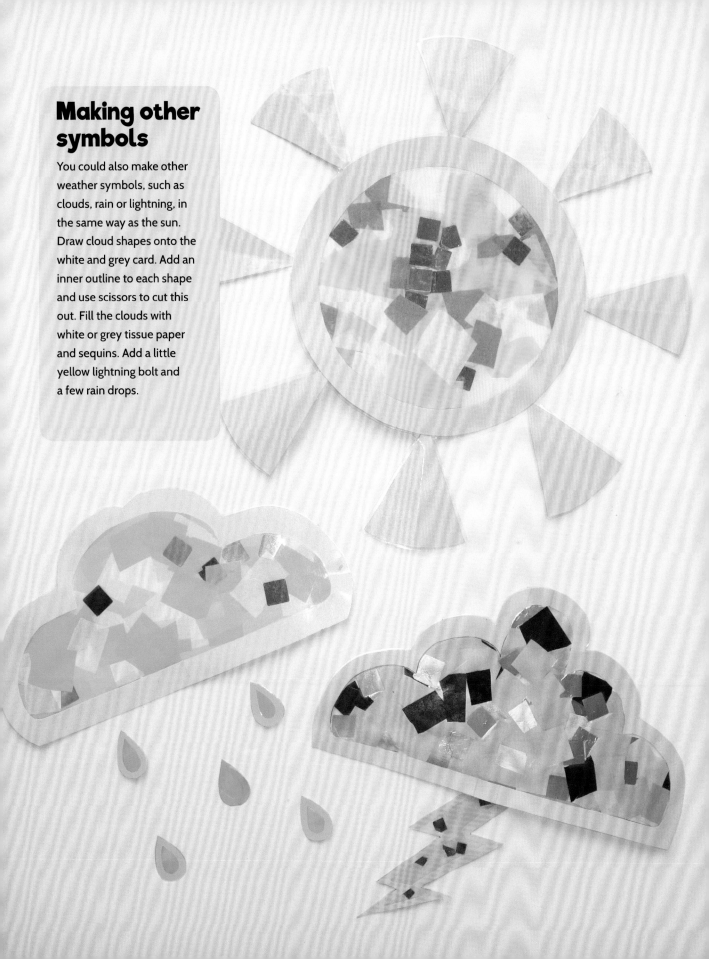

40 Mini piñata

This mini piñata is made from a cardboard tube and is perfect for a party with friends. You could make a heap of them and add different treats inside each one!

You will need

Small cardboard tube
A4 coloured card sheet
Pen or pencil
Scissors

Masking tape
A4 coloured paper sheet
Glue stick
Coloured tissue paper
String or thread

1 Place the tube upright on the card and draw round the end. Draw a second circle, roughly ½in (1cm) larger, around the first circle. You can do this freehand as it doesn't need to be too neat! Cut out the outer circle, then snip inwards all the way around it.

2 Fold up the little tabs and fit the circle over the end of the tube. Wrap masking tape round to secure it.

3 Cut out a rectangle of coloured paper large enough to fit around the tube with a little overlap. Cover the tube with glue and stick the paper in place.

4 Cut strips of coloured tissue paper 1in (2.5cm) wide and long enough to wrap around the tube. Snip fringing along the length of the strips.

5 Glue the strips around the tube, starting at the closed end. Overlap each strip as you work towards the open end.

6 Tape a loop of string inside the open end of the tube. Fill it with goodies such as small toys, stickers, raisins or a few sweets and hang it up. Then use a wooden spoon or piece of dowel to whack it until it bursts!

Coaster bug game

This project provides two fun outdoor games in one – giant tic tac toe (or noughts and crosses) and a bug toss game. Make a target for the bug toss by decorating a box like the one shown here; or place a hoop on the ground for a landing area.

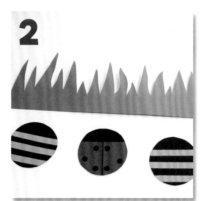

1 Paint one third of each coaster black for the bug's head. Paint yellow and black stripes across five coasters to create bees. Paint the remaining five red and leave to dry before adding a black central line and spots to create ladybirds. Glue googly eyes onto the head end of each coaster.

2 To make the target, cut and trim four strips of green card to look like grass. Paint the box white and then glue the grass border around the base. Cut out a few ladybirds and bees from the coloured card and then glue them onto the box.

You will need
10 cork coasters
Acrylic paint in black, red, white and yellow
Paintbrush
20 googly eyes
Strong glue
Small cardboard box or shoebox without lid for a target
A4 card in red, green, black and yellow

Bug toss
(two players or teams)

Place the target box on the ground. One team has bees, the other has ladybirds. Use a stick to mark where to throw from (start near and move back gradually). The players take turns to see how many bugs they can toss into the box.

Bug tic tac toe
(two players)

One player has the bees, the other has the ladybirds. Lay out four long sticks in the form of a nine-square grid. Each player takes it in turn to place their bug on the grid. The winner is the first to get three of their bugs in a row either up, down or diagonally.

Ice painting

Storing a tray of coloured ice in the freezer makes this a great last-minute activity for a warm day.

You will need
Ice-cube tray
Selection of food colourings
15 lollipop sticks
Freezer
Thick paper or card

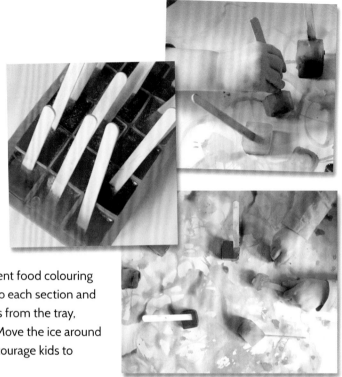

Fill the ice-cube tray with water and mix a different food colouring into each compartment. Place a lollipop stick into each section and leave overnight in the freezer. Remove the cubes from the tray, cover up clothes and surfaces and get painting! Move the ice around the paper or card using the lollipop stick and encourage kids to blend and create patterns with the colours.

Mud-pie kitchen

An outdoor mud-pie kitchen offers children a way to connect with nature, get messy, engage in imaginative role play and conjure up some creative recipes!

You will need
Cooking utensils (real or play versions)
Pots, pans, bowls and cupcake trays
Cupcake cases
Watering can or jug of water
Bucket of compost/soil
Pebbles, flowers, twigs, feathers etc.

Set up your kitchen on a low bench, table or box and stock it with cooking utensils, pots, pans and bowls. Gather ingredients from things you find around you – twigs make great teaspoons, stones can be biscuits or sugar lumps, while buttercups and daisies make lovely cake sprinkles. Use a cupcake tray lined with cupcake cases to serve up mud cakes. Make a little sign and your kitchen is open for business. Wear old clothes and don't forget to wash your hands after making your yummy mud cakes!

Balloon tennis

Using a balloon instead of a ball is perfect for tiny tennis players as the balloon is a lot slower than a ball, making it easier to get a rally going.

You will need (for two players)
2 paper plates
Child-friendly paint or colouring pens
    and stickers
2 lollipop sticks
Duct tape
A balloon

Colour in the plates using paints or colouring pens and then decorate with stickers. Leave them to dry fully. Tape the lollipop sticks onto the back of the plates to create handles. Then blow up the balloon and you're ready for play!

44

Painting with water guns

45

Instead of having a water fight, kids can use water guns to create art. Wearing old clothes (for you and them) for this project is advised as the paint is likely to go everywhere!

Pour a small amount of paint into each water gun and dilute it with water. Tape the canvas or paper to an outside wall. (You may want to cover the surrounding bits of wall first!) Then simply aim and fire! Experiment by using different sprays on a variety of settings – the effects will range from fine mist to big splodges. Kids can get a little messy doing this activity, so it's best to pop an apron on them or have them in old clothes.

You will need
3–4 water guns or spray
    bottles
Child-friendly paints
Water
Canvas or sheet of paper
Clear tape
An outside wall
Old clothes or apron

46 Texture rubbings

You will need
Paper
Coins or other embossed
  or textured flat objects
Chunky wax crayons with
  paper wrappers removed

This quick and easy art activity is a great way to occupy kids when you are out and about. Go on a hunt for textured objects and then relax in a cafe while they are busy making their rubbings.

Place the paper on top of your object and the crayon flat-side down on the paper. Then rub the crayon across the object and watch the imprint appear. Go back and forth over it a few times if you want a darker image. Be experimental – rub over a single object in several colours or move it around under the paper. You can also use a variety of objects for lots of different textures.

Great objects for texture

Flat objects work best. Look around you at home or outdoors and make a collection of items, such as:

• Coins
• Tree bark
• Small, flat grater

• Plaques or door numbers
• Combs
• Leaves and twigs

Paper spinner

This spinner is a bit like a horizontal yo-yo. It might take a little practice, but once you get the rhythm it can whizz for ages.

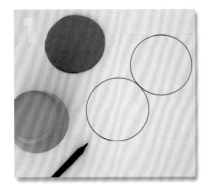

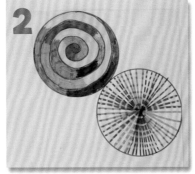

You will need
4–6in (10–15cm)
   diameter bowl
Corrugated card
Colouring pens
Scissors
A4 white card
Glue stick
35in (90cm) length of string
Pen or pencil

1 Place the upturned bowl on the corrugated card, draw around it and cut out a circle. Then place the bowl on the white card and draw two more circles.

2 Colour and cut out the white card circles. These are the spinners – so colourful spirals and circle patterns will work well.

3 Glue the coloured circles onto either side of the corrugated card. Use a pen or pencil point to poke two small holes through the centre. Thread the string through the holes. Knot the ends together and slide your spinner to the centre.

4 Hold the ends of the string and wind up the spinner by looping it over and over. Then pull the ends taut and watch it whoosh! Relax the string before winding it up again. Now keep going and see how many spins you can get.

Card kite

48

You will need
12in (30cm) square of
    coloured card
Pencil and ruler
Scissors
Card scraps in two
    other colours
10 bendy straws
Masking tape
4 lengths of ribbon each
    about 22in (56cm)
7 wooden skewers
    (with pointy ends cut off)
Glue stick
Child-friendly paints
Paintbrush
Empty cardboard ribbon
    spool, about 2.5in (6cm)
    in diameter
13ft (4m) of string
Strong glue

Little ones will have fun decorating and flying this kite. If there's not enough wind to fly it, then it will also make a nice piece of wall art! If you can't find a ribbon spool, you can always make your own. Drill a hole in a jam-jar lid, cut two circular pieces of card $^1/_2$in (1cm) larger than the lid and attach them to either side.

1 Photocopy the template to the size stated and use it to draw the kite shape onto the square of card. Cut it out.

2 Decorate the front of the kite. You could add coloured card triangles and decorative tape detailing as shown, or paint and embellish it with stickers, sequins or ribbon scraps.

3 To make the frame, arrange and cut the bendy straws to fit neatly around the edge of the kite and in a central cross shape. You may need to tape a few straws together, so they match the same lengths as the kite sides.

4 Push a wooden skewer inside each straw, trimming the skewers to the same length as the straws as you go. Then tape the frame together where the straws meet. Tape the four ribbon pieces onto the back of the kite, at the base, for the tail. Trim, so the ribbons are slightly different lengths. Use strong glue to stick the front of the kite onto the frame and then leave it to dry.

5 To make the reel, push a skewer inside a straw and cover it with masking tape. Paint the ribbon spool and the straw yellow. When dry, feed the straw through the centre of the spool for a handle. Wrap a 15in (38cm) length of string around the handle on either side of the reel. Add a dab of strong glue to the string end to keep it in place and stop the reel falling off.

6 Attach one end of the remainder of the string onto the reel using the strong glue. Once the glue is dry, wrap the rest of the string around the reel and tie the other end firmly onto the middle of the kite frame.

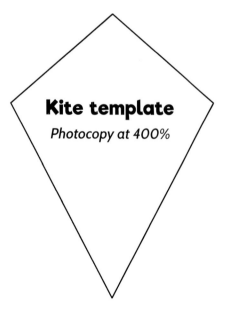

Kite template
Photocopy at 400%

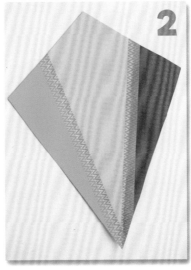

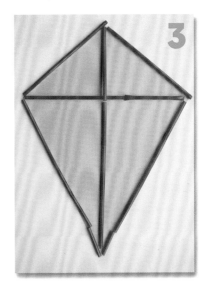

Fly the kite

Unwrap some of the string and ask a grown-up to hold the kite up high. When you feel a breeze let it go, running into the wind to make it fly and dance. You need to keep moving to keep the kite in the air. Even if the kite doesn't stay in the air for long, trying is great fun!

Squirty chalk paint

This super-messy outdoor paint creates wonderfully bright pictures on corrugated card or paving slabs. The rain will probably wash it away, but it may need a little scrub to remove the residue from the cornflour.

**You will need
(for each colour)**
½ cup cornflour
¼ cup flour
Plastic jug
½–¾ cup water
1 tbsp child-friendly paint
1 empty squeezy bottle

Recycle squeezy sauce bottles or find empty ones online.

Measure out the cornflour and flour into a jug. Gradually add the water until you have a thin, easily pourable batter. Add the paint and stir well, then pour the mixture into the bottle. Give it a good shake and you're ready to squirt some art! If you're painting onto card, bear in mind the finished product won't be long lasting, as once it dries the flour will cause the paint to crumble away.

72

Splat painting

50

Experimenting with paint is always fun. The splatting can get quite messy (even in a very small space!) so make sure children wear old clothes or a long-sleeved apron.

You will need
Scissors
Sheet of paper
Deep-sided box or tray (shoe boxes work well)
4–5 large rubber bands
Child-friendly paints
Paintbrush

1 Cut the paper to fit snugly into the base of your box or tray. Fit the rubber bands around the box, spacing them evenly.

2 Spread a generous amount of paint on the underside of each rubber band using the paintbrush. Choose different colours for each band.

3 Now pull each band, aim and let go! The colours will flick onto the paper below. Add more paint when needed and watch your splat painting build up.

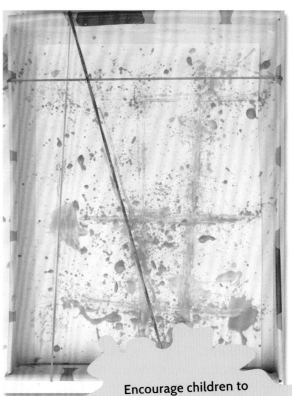

Encourage children to experiment. See what happens if you vary the angle of the rubber bands or move them around the box.

51

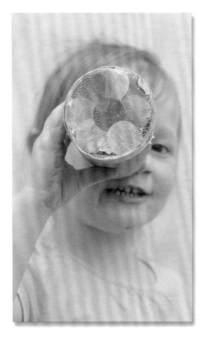

Kaleidoscope

This simple kaleidoscope works best when it is held up to the light. Move the tube around to see the pretty colours, glitter and sequins dance around.

1 Measure across one end of the tube as shown, a few millimetres in from the edge.

2 Cut out three pieces of silver card to this width and ½in (1cm) shorter than the length of the tube.

3 With the silver side on the inside, join the three card pieces into a triangle with masking tape.

4 Slide the triangle into the cardboard tube.

5 Draw around the base of the cardboard tube onto the acetate. Then draw a second circle, about ¼in (5mm) wider, around the first. Cut around the outer circle and snip evenly spaced tabs towards the inner circle. Fold the tabs up. Repeat this step to make a second tabbed circle. With the tabs facing out, push one circle about ½in (1cm) into one end of the tube.

6 Tape torn or cut out tissue-paper shapes onto the inside of the second circle, making sure the tabs are towards you. Pour a sprinkle of glitter and sequins into the circle.

7 Seal the circle into the tube by taping the tabs onto the outside using masking tape.

8 Draw around the other end of the tube onto the black card. Cut out a tabbed circle as before. Snip a tiny peephole at the centre and then attach the circle onto the outside of the tube using masking tape.

9 Glue coloured paper around the tube and then decorate it with stickers, sequins or pretty, patterned tape.

You will need
Cardboard tube
Ruler, pencil and scissors
A4 sheet of reflective
 silver card
A4 sheet of acetate or
 clear plastic
A4 sheet of coloured paper
Masking tape
Coloured tissue-paper scraps
Glitter and sequins
Scrap of black card, about
 3½ x 3½in (9 x 9cm)
Glue stick
Pretty, patterned tape

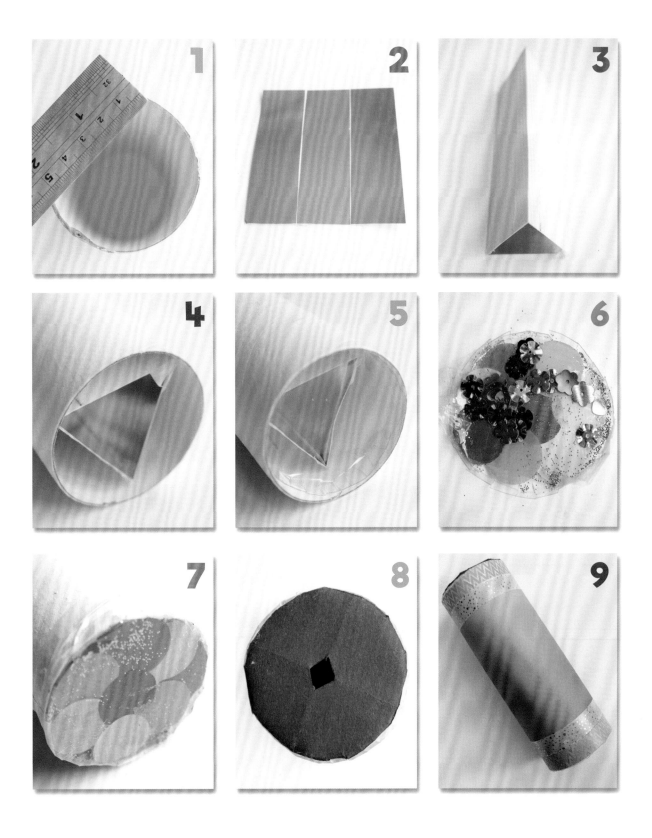

Little laboratory

52 Baking soda bubbles

When baking powder and vinegar meet, they create a huge burst of fizz, which is fun to create, especially if you add food colouring to the vinegar. You can either add the baking soda to the vinegar or vice versa – both produce super fizzes, just in slightly different ways.

You will need
White vinegar
Liquid food colouring
Plastic cups
Teaspoon
Baking powder or soda
Tray
Pipette or teaspoon
Ice-cube tray

1 Pour vinegar into 4 or 5 cups, about 3–4 tablespoons per cup. Add a few drops of food colouring to each cup and stir well.

2 Place the cups on the tray and use a teaspoon to add baking powder to the vinegar. The two will react quickly, creating a colourful fizz of bubbles.

3 Now try it the other way round. Pour vinegar into an ice-cube tray and add a few drops of food colouring to each section. Put a few tablespoons of baking powder in a flat layer into a shallow dish. Dip the pipette into the ice-cube tray and then squirt the coloured vinegar onto the powder. Watch how the colours fizz and blend!

Fizzing fish

These sparkly, mini bath bombs are easy to make and will provide lots of fizzy bathtime fun. You can buy Epsom salts from most pharmacies and citric acid is easily found online.

53

You will need
½ cup bicarbonate of soda
½ cup corn starch
¼ cup Epsom salts
¼ cup citric acid
Few tsp glitter
Mixing bowl
Spoon
4 tsp coconut oil
Liquid food colouring
Small spray-bottle of water
Fish-shape silicone moulds
Whisk

Experiment with different-shaped moulds, but avoid ones with narrow parts as the bath bombs will break as you remove them.

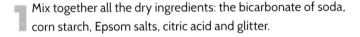

1 Mix together all the dry ingredients: the bicarbonate of soda, corn starch, Epsom salts, citric acid and glitter.

2 Melt the coconut oil in the microwave in short ten-second bursts, until it's a liquid. Add a few drops of food colouring and mix well. For a more intense colour, add a few more drops of food colouring but then less water at the next step.

3 Add the coconut oil and food colouring mixture a little at a time to the dry ingredients and whisk together. Don't add too much liquid at once – this will trigger the fizzing chemical reaction!

4 Add about 10 sprays of water (fewer if you added extra food colouring earlier), whisking continuously after each spray, until you have a clumpy mixture that holds together. If the mixture isn't clumping, add more sprays of water until it does. Press the mixture into the silicone mould so that it's tightly packed.

5 Leave to dry in the moulds overnight, then carefully remove.

6 Drop the fish into a bowl of warm water and watch as they fizz!

54

Giant ice marbles

These marbles can leak a little bit of colour once frozen so wear old clothes when playing with them, and wear rubber gloves to protect your hands from staining.

This is a great activity for an icy day. Leave your filled balloons outdoors overnight to freeze, or pop them in your freezer if it isn't cold enough outside. Just bear in mind the size when you are making them – large ones could easily fill your freezer!

1 Use a cocktail stick to place a little food colouring inside the neck of the balloons. If you want an intense colour add a little more, bearing in mind that the colour will eventually leach from the marble. Attach each balloon to the cold tap. Gently fill them with water until about 6in (15cm) in diameter. Then remove and knot the end and freeze overnight.

2 Once frozen, snip away the balloons to reveal icy giant marbles. It's a good idea to wear rubber gloves and old clothes in case of any staining as the ice starts to melt.

You will need
4 balloons
Different gel food colourings
4 cocktail sticks or wooden skewers
Water
Scissors

Frozen marble fun

Play with the marbles like real marbles, by picking a 'shooter' to bowl at the rest, or use them like bowling balls to knock down some stick skittles.

Uncoloured giant marbles work just as well, so skip the colour if you're worried about staining clothes and hands. You could even add glitter or sequins instead to the balloon before freezing.

When play is over, these giant ice marbles are great fun to smash (make sure to throw them away from people), or you can pour warm water over them and watch them disappear.

Waterproof sand

55

You will need
5–6 cups play sand
Fabric protector spray
Tray

This sand is completely waterproof - pour it into a bowl of water and it will form silvery worms of sand that, when scooped out, should be completely dry. It's great fun to play with and easy-peasy to make.

Spread the sand on a tray and spray it all over with fabric protector. Stir it around and spray again. Keep going until the sand is thoroughly damp, then leave it to dry out completely. Now you can play with it! Try pouring it into water and building your own underwater landscape. You can also pour water onto the sand and watch it form little droplets.

Giant bubbles

These giant bubbles are endless fun on a sunny day. You can pick up the guar gum from a health-food shop. This is definitely an activity for outside as the bubble solution will drip liberally from the wand!

56

**You will need
(for the solution)**
½ cup washing-up liquid
Large plastic bowl
Whisk
2 tsp guar gum
2 tsp baking powder
4¼ pints (2 litres) water
(for the wand)
2 short lengths of dowel
   or wooden chopsticks
2 eye-hooks
85in (2.2m) string
Small nut or bolt (weight)

The guar gum isn't essential but it strengthens the surface tension and makes the bubbles last longer. Make the mixture a day in advance for even stronger bubbles.

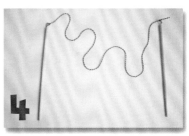

1 Pour the washing-up liquid, baking powder and guar gum into the bowl and mix it together with a whisk.

2 Pour in the water and mix together. Leave the mixture for a few hours, or overnight, to thicken and settle.

3 Screw the eye-hooks into one end of each dowel.

4 Cut three lengths of string, one 35in (90cm) and two 25in (65cm). Tie both ends of the longer string onto the eye-hooks.

5 Tie one end of each short string onto an eye-hook. Tie the other ends onto your weight. You should now have a string triangle between the dowels.

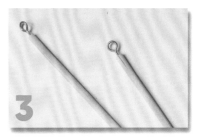

6 Hold the dowels together with the hanging weight below them and dip the string triangle slowly into the solution. Pull it out, open the dowels and blow or swing the wand to release your giant bubbles!

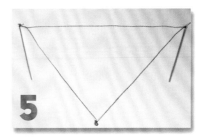

57 Flying planes

These paper planes are propelled with air blown through a straw. You could adapt this design really easily to make anything else fly – a bird, a rocket or even a superhero. Make a few and see who can fly the furthest!

You will need
A4 sheet of scrap paper
A4 sheet of corrugated card
A4 sheet of coloured card
Pencil and scissors
Glue stick
Colouring pens
Ruler
Clear tape
Plastic straw

1 Draw and cut out a simple aeroplane template, about 7in (17cm) long, onto the scrap paper. Draw around the template onto the corrugated and coloured card and cut both out.

2 Glue the coloured card shape on top of the corrugated card shape and decorate your plane using colouring pens.

3 Measure and draw a 4 x 1in (10 x 2.5cm) rectangle onto the leftover coloured card. Add ½in (1cm) tabs along each long side and one short side. Cut out the rectangle, fold along the tab lines and tape it together.

4 Tape the box on top of the plane. Place it centrally, with the open end towards the tail. To fly, insert a straw into the open end of the box and blow hard. Have a race to see who can blow their plane the furthest!

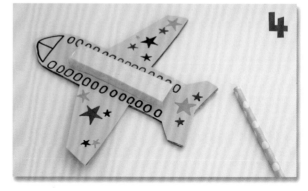

DIY chalk

58

Did you know that you can make your own chalk? And it's easy! This chalk is made into giant sticks, which is great for little hands to grab hold of, and perfect for pavements and patios. You can create a giant masterpiece and then let the rain wash it off.

You will need (for 6 giant pieces)
3 A4 acetate sheets
Scissors
Duct tape
Large lump of play dough
Tray
9oz (240g) plaster of Paris
Small bowls
Metal spoons
Water
Poster paint in 6 colours

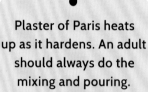

!

Plaster of Paris heats up as it hardens. An adult should always do the mixing and pouring. Do not put into direct contact with skin.

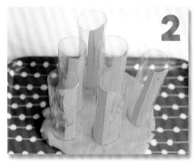

1 For the moulds, cut out six acetate squares each 5 x 5in (12 x 12cm). Roll each square into a tube, leaving an overlap of about 1in (2cm). Tape the edge to seal.

2 Roll out a 1in (2cm) thick circle of play dough. Transfer it onto a tray or board and push in the upright acetate tubes.

3 For each chalk stick, measure 1½oz (40g) plaster of Paris into a bowl. In another bowl or a cup, mix 2fl.oz (60ml) water with 1 tbsp paint. Add this to the plaster of Paris and mix thoroughly.

4 Then spoon the mixture into a tube. Once full, use the end of the spoon to prod away any gaps and air bubbles in the mixture.

5 Repeat steps 3 and 4 to make the other five chalks. Set them aside to harden overnight, then remove the acetate and allow them to fully dry. The chalk will be usable, but probably still a little damp, after 24 hours. For best results, leave for a couple of days.

59

Secret messages

This a great project that allows kids to write secret messages or draw pictures using a wax candle. The art is then revealed with a few strokes of paint.

You will need
Long white candle
Thick paper
Watercolour paints
Paintbrush

Use the end of the candle to write or draw a message or picture onto the paper. Make it simple as it's not very easy to see what you're doing. (You can hold the paper up to the light if you want to check what you've done.) Mix the paints with plenty of water so that they are runny – then paint over the paper to expose a hidden surprise!

60

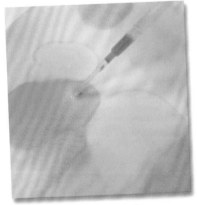

Milk marbling

When washing-up liquid is added to milk it reacts with the proteins and fat, causing the milk to dart around. Adding food colouring allows you to see this reaction and the marbling effect it creates.

You will need
Full-fat milk and large bowl
Liquid food colouring
Pipette or teaspoon
Cocktail stick
Washing-up liquid
Watercolour paper

Pour the milk into a large bowl and add a few drops of food colouring using a pipette or teaspoon. Dip a cocktail stick into washing-up liquid and place the end in the milk. Watch the food colouring jump away from the cocktail stick and create a marbled effect. The more often you dip the stick into the washing-up liquid, the more the mixture marbles. It's mesmerizing! To keep the marbling as a piece of art, rest a piece of watercolour paper on top of the milk and then gently peel it off and leave to dry.

DIY light box

The lights and shapes in this sensory activity will fascinate young children, and older kids will enjoy combining them to make pictures.

You will need
Large clear plastic box with lid
Aluminium foil
Coloured tissue paper
Scissors
Laminating sheets or contact paper
Battery-operated fairy lights

Line the base and two sides of the box with foil, folding it over the rim to keep it in place. Cut the tissue paper into lots of different shapes, laminating or sealing them between contact paper sheets. Fill the box with fairy lights and switch on. Fit the lid on the box and stack the translucent tissue shapes on top ready for some magical picture making.

61

Paint
and print

62 Veggie-print paper

Printing with fruit and vegetables adds a personal touch to wrapping paper and is a great way to use up old veggies. Cut shapes and silhouettes into half a potato or experiment with other fresh produce to create unusual patterns and textures.

You will need
Brown wrapping paper
Scissors
Vegetables and fruit
Knife
Kitchen towel
Child-friendly paints
Sponge or paintbrush
Scrap paper

1 Cut a large sheet of brown paper and select your vegetables and fruit. Chop them to create an effective stamping surface and to be easy to handle. Dab your stampers with kitchen towel to remove excess moisture.

2 Spread paint over the surface of your stamper using a sponge or paintbrush – or dip it directly into the paint for more of a splodge!

3 Try a few test stamps on scrap paper before stamping a design onto the brown sheet. Experiment with different colours and vegetables to create a nice repeating pattern.

Best stampers

APPLES AND PEARS Cut in half from the stem for a classic shape.
CELERY Cut 2in (5cm) from the bottom of a bunch and use the base to create a flower-like pattern.
PEPPERS AND ONIONS Great for shape and pattern when sliced through the centre.
BROCCOLI AND CAULIFLOWER Use as a speckled stamp or slice through a cross section for 'trees'.
CITRUS FRUITS Make sure to remove excess juice before stamping.

Foam stamps

Kids will enjoy being able to draw out their own stamp designs for this simple activity. Use the stamps with ink pads or paint – the latter will give a splodgier effect. Once you are done, wipe the stamps clean ready to use again!

You will need (for 10-15 stamps)
A4 sheet of craft foam
Scissors
Double-sided tape
Pen or pencil
Corrugated card
Duct or masking tape, about 1½in (4cm) wide
Child-friendly paints or ink pad

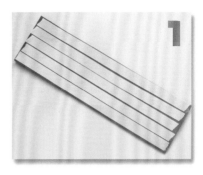

1 Measuring from the top of the sheet, cut a 3in (7.5cm) foam rectangle. Attach strips of double-sided tape on one side to completely cover the whole surface.

2 On the other side of the foam draw the outlines of 10–15 simple shapes, about 1½in (4cm) in size. Cut these out.

3 Measure and cut out 2in (5cm) squares from corrugated card, one for each foam shape. Peel off the foam backing from the shapes and stick them onto the card squares.

4 Cut off 2½in (6cm) lengths of duct tape and pinch them in the centre to form a little handle. Stick them onto the back of each stamp.

5 Press the stamps onto an ink pad or apply paint with a brush and then get stamping!

64 Ziplock bag painting

This is a no-mess way for really young kids to experiment with paint and colour mixing. Try to pick paint colours that will blend well together rather than end up as a murky brown, such as red, pink and yellow, or blue, green and yellow.

You will need
Child-friendly paint in
   three or four colours
Ziplock bag
Clear tape

Lay a ziplock bag flat and squeeze three or four paint colours into it, keeping them apart if you can. Press the bag lightly all over to eliminate air then seal it. Tape the bag to a window or door pane and let your child move the paint around and create patterns against the glass.

Toy tracks printing

This is a great first art project and a fun, quick way to create patterns and prints using plastic toys instead of paintbrushes. Go for cars with treads on the wheels or animal models that will make interesting footprints.

You will need
Child-friendly paint
Plastic plates or trays
3–4 plastic model cars
    or animals
Paper or card

Use a different colour paint for each toy. Pour the paints onto the plates or trays. Wheel the cars or stamp the animals through the paint and then drive or walk them across the paper or card.

66 Cling-film watercolour

Cling film creates an interesting effect when added on top of paint. Make sure the paint is runny and applied liberally so that the cling film can pick it up.

 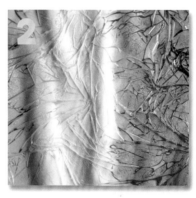 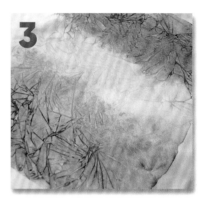

You will need

Watercolour paints in different colours
Water
3–4 plastic cups
Large sheet of card
Paintbrushes
Cling film

1 Put a teaspoon of paint into each cup. Then thin the paint by stirring in 3 tbsp of water.

2 Paint the card liberally with the colours, so that they touch and blend a little but don't mix. The card needs to be wet with paint for the cling film to pick up the colours.

3 Gently place a large sheet of cling film over the card. You will see the colours cling to it immediately! Pinch and move the film around a little, so that the colours blend and lattice-like networks form. Then leave it to dry overnight before removing the film to reveal your masterpiece!

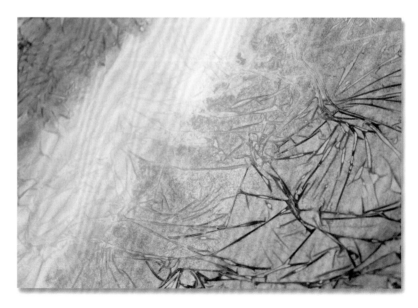

Try spelling out names and words or creating other kinds of masking-tape shapes.

Masking-tape reveal

This dazzling geometric design can be created with even the smallest of tots. Paint over the tape and peel away to reveal your painted masterpiece.

You will need
Art canvas or card
Masking or painter's tape
Child-friendly paint and paintbrush
Glitter

1 Divide the canvas into sections using strips of masking tape.

2 Paint each section a different colour, or paint a mixture of colours across the entire canvas. Don't worry about getting paint on the tape.

3 Sprinkle glitter over a few sections while the paint is still wet. Once the paint is dry, tap off the excess glitter and peel away the tape.

Pompom peg art

Versatile fluffy pompoms can be used for all kinds of crafts. For a quick paint project, clip one onto the end of a clothes peg and use it to create a colourful dot picture.

You will need
Child-friendly paint
Plate
Pompoms in different sizes
Clothes pegs
Plain white paper

Put thick dollops of paint onto the plate and clip the pompoms onto the pegs. Then dip your pompom into the paint and onto the page. You can use different pompoms for each colour or add a mixture of colours onto each one.

Other peg-printing ideas

There are lots of other things besides pompoms that work brilliantly for printing with pegs. Try using cut-up bits of sponge, cotton wool, bundles of string or fabric scraps. You could also attach flowerheads to the peg. If you spread the paint thinly onto the petals with a paintbrush they will leave a nice imprint once pressed down onto a piece of paper.

69 Firework painting

Create a pretty firework display by first crayoning and then painting onto a sheet of paper, before scraping away the topcoat to reveal colourful booms, fizzes and whizzes in a dark night sky.

You will need
Wax crayons
Black acrylic paint
Paintbrush
Plain white paper
Wooden skewer or cocktail stick (with ends
    cut off) or the end of a thin paintbrush

1 Using the wax crayons, cover the sheet of paper in blocks of colour.

2 Paint a thin layer of black acrylic paint on top and leave to dry.

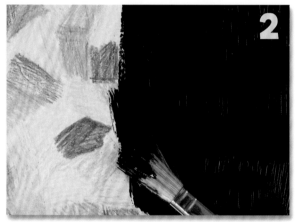

3 Now use the skewer or cocktail stick to draw lots of fireworks whizzing through the sky, scraping away the black paint as you go.

Rolling-pin art

70

You can make all sorts of wonderful printed patterns by taping textured items onto a rolling pin. Bubble wrap, hook-and-loop tape (Velcro), foam shapes or balls of sticky tack all work well.

You will need
Child's rolling pin
Cling film
Clear tape
String, bubble wrap or other textural items
Child-friendly paints and paintbrushes
Paper

Wrap the rolling pin in cling film and secure it with tape at each end. Then wrap a length of string around it on top of the cling film. Secure it with tape, brush paint all over the pin and then roll it along the paper. Try blending other colours into the string, or adding patches of paint to the rolling pin.

Feather painting

71

This is a fascinating way to experiment with printing, pattern building and colour. A larger feather works best as it can hold more paint and the sturdy quill makes it easier to handle.

You can buy feathers at craft stores, but it's much more fun to get your wellies on and go on an outdoor feather hunt.

You will need
Feathers in different sizes
Child-friendly paints
Paintbrush
Paper

Use the paintbrush to spread paint thinly over one side of a feather. Paint two or three sections in different colours. Gently press the painted side of the feather onto the paper. Peel it off, apply more paint and press the feather down again onto another part of the paper to build up an abstract picture.

72 Puffy paint

This paint has a lovely foamy texture and stays puffy after it sets. It is perfect for creating 3D pictures of rainbows, houses or any other basic shapes you like.

You will need
3 cups shaving foam
1 cup flour
1 cup glue
Large bowl
Metal spoon
3-4 liquid food colourings
3-4 small bowls
3-4 ziplock bags
Scissors
Paper or card

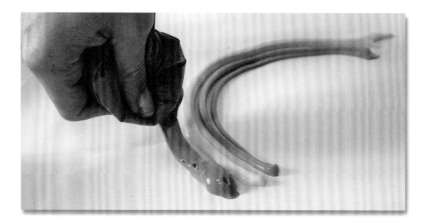

Mix together the shaving foam, flour and glue with a metal spoon. Try not to overmix or the foam will lose puffiness. Divide the mix among the small bowls and stir a different food colouring into each one. Spoon the paint into ziplock bags, eliminating most of the air before sealing them. Make a small snip at the corner of each bag. Now pipe your picture onto the paper. It can be left to dry but it is likely to lose some of its puffiness.

73 Tissue-paper artwork

This is a simple way to create a colourful piece of artwork without paints. Adding water to the tissue paper causes the colour to bleed onto the canvas, leaving a paler imprint behind.

You will need
Coloured tissue paper
Scissors
An art canvas
Water
Paintbrush

Cut the tissue paper into different-sized shapes. Brush water onto the canvas. Arrange the tissue-paper shapes on the canvas and paint another layer of water on top. Leave it to dry completely and then peel off the tissue paper to reveal the imprint.

Foil butterfly

Aluminium foil makes a fun alternative surface to paper and adds a lovely shiny effect to pictures. For extra sparkle, sprinkle your picture with glitter before leaving it to dry.

You will need
Aluminium foil
Scissors
Child-friendly paints
Glitter (optional)
Cotton buds
Pencil

Cut a sheet of foil and smooth it flat onto the table. Foil can tear easily, so use cotton buds instead of a paintbrush to apply your colours. Create a symmetrical print by painting on one half of the foil sheet, folding it in half and then carefully opening it out again. Once the paint is dry, refold the foil and draw an outline of half a butterfly on the fold. Cut out the shape then open up.

Playing
and
performing

75 Paper-cup puppet

You will need
1 paper coffee cup
1 paper espresso cup
Acrylic silver paint
Paintbrush
Red embroidery thread
    and needle
Scissors
Handful of pony beads
    (approx. 40 beads)
8–10 buttons in varying sizes
Silver card sheet
Coloured card scraps in silver,
    red, white and black
Clear tape
Strong glue
Double-sided tape
Black colouring pen
2 googly eyes
Lollipop stick
Black pipe cleaner

This cute robot is upcycled from two paper cups. He can be painted and decorated by kids and then turned into a dancing robot.

1 Paint both cups with silver paint. This may take a few coats to get an even coverage.

2 Use a needle to make two holes in the bottom of the large cup. Cut a 20in (50cm) length of red embroidery thread. Tie a button onto one end and thread 10 pony beads on top. Thread a needle onto the other end of the thread. Starting inside the cup, push the needle up through one hole and down through the other. Pull the thread until the beads and button are visible below the rim. Then thread 10 beads onto the other end and tie a matching button onto the end.

3 Make a hole in either side of the large cup, about 1½in (4cm) from the base. Cut a 30in (76cm) length of thread. Tie a button about 10in (25cm) from one end and thread nine beads next to it. Use a needle to thread this armpiece into one side hole and out through the other. Thread on nine beads followed by a button, knotted to secure, about 10in (25cm) from the other end.

4 For the control panel, cut out a square of red card, about 2 x 2in (5 x 5cm). Cut out some smaller panels from different black and silver card scraps and glue in place, along with a few buttons or beads. Use double-sided tape to stick the control panel onto the large cup.

5 For the antenna, bend the pipe cleaner into a small triangle, leaving about 2in (5cm) excess at each end. Push the ends through the base of the small cup, twisting them to secure. Cut a rectangle from white card for a mouth, adding lines for teeth. Tape it to the smaller cup and then stick on googly eyes. Pop the head on top of the body cup. It should fit snugly, but use a little tape or glue for stability if you like.

6 Tie the threads from the arms onto the lollipop stick, about ½in (1cm) from either end. Loop a thread length through the antenna and knot it around the centre of the stick.

76 Peg monsters

These chatty little monsters are quick, easy and need few materials. They are attached to pegs and split at the mouth, so can be made to talk whenever you squeeze the peg open.

You will need
(for one monster)
Wooden clothes peg
Coloured card
Ruler
Colouring pens
Scissors
Double-sided tape
Scrap of white card

1 Place the peg onto the coloured card. Measure the section that opens and draw a line this length. This marks the position of the monster's mouth.

2 Draw a monster's face around the line. Draw the nose, eyes and ears above the line, with the chin below it. The line (mouth) must stretch right across the face. Colour in the monster's face.

3 Cut around the face and snip across the line to create two pieces. For teeth, cut a zigzag strip of white card and tape it behind the top piece.

4 Attach the pieces to the peg using the doubled-sided tape, so that the top piece slightly overlaps the bottom piece. If you find that the teeth catch, bend them slightly outwards.

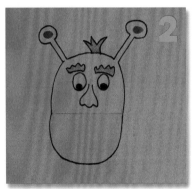

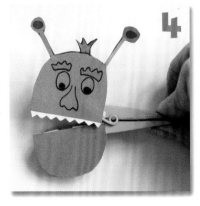

Rattle drum

Kids will love getting messy making this drum as it involves papier mâché. Bear in mind that this will need to dry overnight, so the activity needs to be done in two parts.

77

You will need
Small circular cardboard container (such as a cheese box)
Needle threaded with string
Scissors
Length of dowel
   (approximately ¼ x 12in/0.5 x 30cm)
PVA glue
Water
A few paintbrushes
Newspaper, torn into 1in (2.5cm) squares
Masking tape
Child-friendly paint
4 buttons or beads

Circular cheese containers are perfect for this activity.

1 Make a small hole by pushing a needle through the side of the container, then make it a bit bigger by wiggling a pair of closed scissors in it. The hole needs to be large enough to fit the dowel through. Push the dowel through to the opposite side. Now push the needle and string through from one side to the other, so they cross the dowel. Use some tape to secure the dowel and string firmly inside the container. Tape on the lid.

2 For the papier mâché paste, mix two parts glue to one part water and spread it over the tub using a paintbrush. Cover the tub with the newspaper pieces, overlapping them so there are no gaps. Leave to dry overnight.

3 Choose your colours and paint the drum in any design you like. Leave it to dry.

4 Thread two buttons onto either end of the string, knotting firmly to keep them in place.

5 Play the drum by twisting the dowel between both hands. Keep the drum at arm's length away from your face.

78

Mermaid mobile

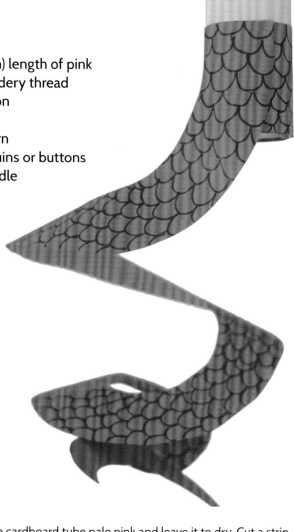

This little mermaid is made from a cardboard tube, with woollen locks of golden hair and a curly tail made from a spiral of card. You can hang her onto your ceiling and watch her twist slowly round.

You will need

Short cardboard tube
Pale pink child-friendly paint
Paintbrush
Scissors
A4 sheet of dark pink card
PVA glue
Colouring pens
Scrap of yellow card

Pencil
8in (20cm) length of pink
   embroidery thread
   or ribbon
Craft glue
Yellow yarn
Shell sequins or buttons
Large needle

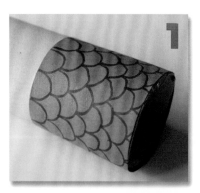

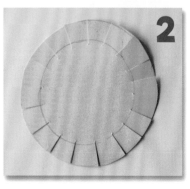

1 Paint the cardboard tube pale pink and leave it to dry. Cut a strip 2 x 8in (5 x 20cm) from the dark-pink card. Cover it with glue and wrap the strip around one end of the tube. Use a darker pink pen to add scales.

2 Place the other end of the tube upright on the yellow card and draw around it. Roughly add an additional ¾in (2cm) around the circle and cut out. Snip tabs around it as shown.

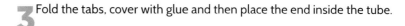

3 Fold the tabs, cover with glue and then place the end inside the tube.

4 Using the rest of the pink card, draw and cut out a spiral about 2½in (6cm) wide. Cut both ends of the spiral straight across. Draw on darker pink scales all over.

5 Fold a scrap of the pink card and draw and cut out half a mermaid tail. Open it out and glue it to the inner spiral end.

6 Snip 6in (15cm) long strands of yellow yarn until you have enough to make the hair. Cover the yellow card tube end in glue, then attach the strands in rows to cover the card completely. Make rows going one way first, then put more glue on top and add another layer with rows going in the opposite direction.

7 Once dry, tie the yarn in two bunches using the embroidery thread or ribbon. Add the mermaid's face using the colouring pens.

8 Glue the spiral onto the tube, on top of the pink card strip. Glue on the sequins or buttons for the bikini top, adding a pink line to connect them.

9 Finally, thread a loop of yellow yarn through the top of the hair so you can hang up the mermaid. Pull the tail a little so that it hangs nicely and twirls a bit.

79 Story stones

Make a set of story stones by drawing out characters, places and objects onto pebbles, which you can either collect from a beach or pick up from a garden centre. If you don't want to draw the pictures, you could also add stickers to the stones; just make sure you add a layer of varnish to hold them in place. Keep the pebbles in a bag and draw them out at random to build a whimsical little tale that will keep little ones enthralled.

You will need
10-15 smooth pebbles
White acrylic spray paint (optional)
Coloured permanent markers
Gloss craft varnish
Paintbrush

1 If you would like the pebbles to be white (you can leave them natural if you prefer), spread them out on a sheet of newspaper outside and spray them with the paint. This should ONLY be done by an adult. Leave the pebbles to dry for about half an hour before flipping them over and spraying on the other side. You can leave the pebbles unpainted if you prefer, but the pictures will show up better on a light surface.

2 Draw a picture on each pebble in permanent marker pen. Cover surfaces and clothing and supervise children using these pens.

3 Brush a thin layer of varnish over the pebbles to seal in the colour and to add some shine.

Permanent markers can stain, so cover surfaces and clothing and supervise children using these pens.

Story stone ideas
CHARACTERS King, queen, mermaid
PLACES Castle, forest, mountain
OBJECTS Key, map, balloon
CREATURES Kangaroo, unicorn, dragon
TRANSPORT Boat, bus, plane
FOOD Ice cream, apple, pizza

Toy watch

Kids love toy clocks and watches and they're a great introduction to numbers and time. This one is made from foam, so it's durable, and it has movable hands for them to practise telling the time.

80

You will need

Circular lid about 1½in (4cm) in diameter	Small split pin
Scraps of card in white and black	Colouring pen
Scissors	Hook-and-loop fastening dots
Scraps of craft foam in gold and blue	Pin
	Sticky tack
	Craft knife

1 Draw around the lid onto the white card. Cut out with scissors and place the card circle on the blue foam. Draw a circle about ¼in (5mm) bigger around the card and cut out. Use the craft knife to cut two 1in (2.5cm) slits in the foam circle, ¾in (2cm) apart.

2 Measure your child's wrist and cut a ¾in (2cm) strip of gold foam to this length, adding 1in (2.5cm) for overlap. Slide the strip through the slits in the foam circle.

3 Add numbers to the card circle for the watch face. Measure to find the centre and mark this in pencil. Put a little sticky tack on the back then poke a small hole through the front using a pin.

4 Measure and cut two watch hands from the black card. They can be straight or have arrowheads. The longer one should be about ¾in (2cm), the shorter one about ½in (1cm). Both should be wide enough to hold the split pin.

5 Poke a hole through the end of each watch hand using the pin. Push the split pin through the smaller hand first, giving it a little twist so it turns. Then push the pin through the bigger hand and twist. Finally, push the split pin through the clock face and open on the back.

6 Glue the watch face to the foam circle and then add a hook-and-loop fastening dot – one on top and one underneath – to either end of the strap.

81

Pompom bee

Pompoms are fun for kids to make and once mastered will give lots of scope for creative makes – from cute rabbits and pretty birds to a strung-together caterpillar or pretty garland. This little bee is made up of two pompoms and decorated with googly eyes and pipe-cleaner wings.

You will need
A4 sheet of card
Pencil
Scissors
Small ball of black yarn
Small ball of yellow yarn
2 googly eyes
Strong glue
1 black pipe cleaner
2 white pipe cleaners

1 Draw two 3in (8cm) diameter circles onto the card. In the centre of each circle draw a smaller 1½in (4cm) circle. Cut them out to leave two doughnut-ring card discs. Place one disc on top of the other.

2 Cut an arm's length of black yarn and wind it around the discs. Then wind an arm's length of yellow yarn next to the black. Continue alternating the black and yellow until you have gone all the way round. Repeat the process with a few more layers, winding black yarn onto black and yellow yarn onto yellow. Continue, until the middle hole is no longer visible. This will make a nice plump pompom.

112

3 Feel for the edge of the card disc and then snip through the yarn all the way around the circle.

4 Cut a 12in (30cm) length of black yarn, slide it in between the two card discs and knot it tightly. Slip off the two discs, fluff up the pompom and give it a little trim to neaten. Leave the long, black yarn strand tied around the middle uncut.

5 Repeat steps 1–4 using just black yarn for the bee's head. You can reuse the cardboard discs, just trimming the pompom so that it's smaller.

6 Join the pompoms by tying the long strand of black yarn from the head around the body. Make sure the long strand of black yarn on the body is at the top and glue a pair of googly eyes onto the head. Twist the black pipe cleaner around the head for the antennae.

7 Bend the two white pipe cleaners into wing shapes and twist them onto the middle of the body.

8 Tie a long length of black yarn around the head and join it to the strand around the body. Hang up your bee and watch him fly!

You can easily make other animals from pompoms! Add pipe-cleaner legs for a spider, make rabbits with felt ears and a mini pompom tail, or string them together for a caterpillar.

113

82 Box camera

Upcycling cardboard boxes into play objects is a brilliant way to reuse them. This cardboard box camera uses a small box, bottle tops and a few other bits and pieces.

1 Remove the contents of your box and reseal it using masking tape. On the A4 card, lay your box on its side and draw around it. Repeat this so you have two rectangles. Cut them out using scissors and use double-sided tape to stick them onto the top and bottom of the box.

2 To cover the rest of the box, place it flat onto the coloured card and cut a strip of card long enough to wrap around the box. Cut this out and use double-sided tape to stick it to the box.

3 To make the wrist strap, cut a 12in (30cm) long strip of ribbon or sequins, fold in half and use decorative tape to stick onto the side of the camera.

4 Decorate the rest of the box using buttons, sequins and decorative tape. Stick a bottle cap on the top with double-sided tape. For the lens, stick a large button on the front and a smaller one on top of it.

You will need
A small cardboard box (such as cereal selection boxes)
A4 sheet coloured card
Pencil and ruler
Scissors
Masking tape
Double-sided tape
12in (30cm) length of narrow ribbon, ric-rac braid or sequin strip
Colourful bottle caps, buttons, sequins, card scraps, decorative tape

Humpty Dumpty egg

Blowing eggs is a fun activity and lots of things can be made from the empty eggs – Easter chicks, decorative ornaments or this little accident-prone fellow.

You will need

Egg
Sharp knife
Bowl
Wooden skewer
Child-friendly paint in green and blue
Permanent markers

Blue plastic bottle top
Cardboard tube
Scrap of blue card
Clear tape
Glue and scissors
A4 sheet of white card
Pencil and ruler

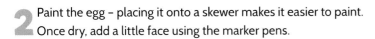

1 An adult should gently insert the tip of a sharp knife into the top of the egg to make a hole. Twist the knife to widen the hole to about ¼in (5mm). Don't worry if the egg cracks a bit. Repeat at the other end of the egg then hold it over a bowl. Put your mouth over the top hole and blow (do NOT suck!) the contents through the bottom hole into the bowl. Rinse and dry.

2 Paint the egg – placing it onto a skewer makes it easier to paint. Once dry, add a little face using the marker pens.

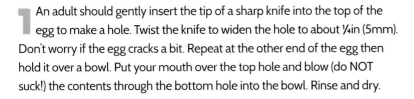

3 For the peak of the hat, place the bottle top onto the blue card and draw halfway around it. Move the top a few millimetres to the side and draw a second line halfway around to make a crescent shape. Cut it out and snip a row of tabs along the inward curve. Fold up the tabs and tape them inside the bottle top, then glue it on top of the egg.

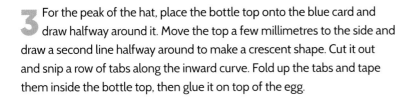

4 For the legs, cut a 1in (2.5cm) wide section from the end of the cardboard tube. Then cut another ¾in (2cm) wide piece and cut it in half. Glue these leg pieces beneath the circular section, as shown. Paint them and leave to dry. Add pockets and other details in pen. Cut out and colour a pair of card shoes and glue them in position. Finally, glue the Humpty egg at the top of the legs.

5 For the wall, measure and cut a rectangle of white card about 10 x 5in (25 x 13cm). In the centre of the long side, draw two parallel lines 1in (2.5cm) apart. Add another parallel line on either side, each ½in (1cm) from each short side. Turn the card over and draw on bricks before folding along the lines, as shown. Cut a rectangle of card for the base, about 2½ x 5in (6 x 13cm). Glue the wall tabs onto it and sit Humpty on his wall.

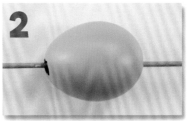

115

Tailor the puppets to your child's interests and create as many as you like, or add to the set later.

Shadow puppet theatre

84

A collection of shadow puppets and a shoebox theatre are really easy to make and great fun to play with. The puppets move behind a tissue-paper screen and are lit by a torch, which projects the scene onto the paper.

You will need
Printer
White paper
Card
Scissors
Glue
Wooden skewers
Duct tape
Shoebox
Pencil and ruler
White tissue paper
Silver paint
Paintbrush
Colouring pens
Torch

1 Look on the Internet for silhouette images of characters – fairy tales work well. Print them out, scaled to about 4in (10cm) high.

2 Roughly cut out the silhouettes, glue them onto the card and then make careful cut-outs.

3 Attach each puppet to a blunt skewer using strong duct tape with the sharp end attached to the top of the puppet so it is concealed.

4 To make the theatre, upend the box and draw a rectangle around the base, 1½in (4cm) in from the edge. Cut it out to leave a frame.

5 Paint the box silver, then tape or glue the tissue paper onto the back of the frame. Decorate your theatre using the colouring pens – being careful of surfaces and clothes!

6 To put on your puppet show, place the theatre on a low table. Position the lit torch about a foot behind the box. Move the puppets around in the light beam between the torch and the theatre and let the show commence! Moving them nearer the light will make the puppets look as though they are moving towards the audience.

85

Magnetic animal mash-up

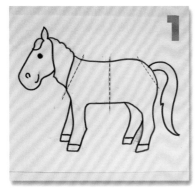

Create some strange new animals and stick them onto your fridge to confuse anyone who walks past. You could also make mixed-up people or monsters if you like, or even a combination of all three.

You will need
4 A4 sheets of white paper
Pencil and ruler
Scissors
Black colouring pen
Pencil and ruler
Scissors
Child-friendly paint
Paintbrush
4 magnetic A4 sheets
Glue stick

1 Choose four animals to use for your mash-up. Try to pick animals with unusual features – such as an elephant, a mouse or a giraffe. Draw the first animal in profile onto the paper, large enough to fill the sheet. Divide the animal into four parts by drawing a pencil line across the neck, another down the middle and a third just in front of the tail. Measure the distance between the lines.

2 Place a second sheet of paper over the first animal and draw another. Use the lines on the first animal as a guide to keep the proportions for the second animal roughly the same. Divide this animal into four parts as before. Follow the same steps to draw two more animals.

3 Paint the animals using different colours for each. Don't worry if the pencil lines disappear. Cut around the animals roughly and glue them, one per sheet, onto the non-magnetic side of the sheets.

4 Cut out the animals and divide each into four pieces, roughly along the pencil lines. If you can't see the lines, check your earlier measurements to make sure you cut in the right places. Now get mixing!

Wooden spoon puppets

A wooden spoon, paint and felt are all you need to make these little people. Recreate your family and friends by using different-sized spoons and lots of colours of felt and paint. If you want an adventure, model your puppets on favourite superheroes or animals.

1 Leaving the handle unpainted, paint the back of each spoon pale pink for the face. For slightly different skin shades, mix the pink with a little white or brown paint. Once dry, use a pencil to draw and then paint the hair onto the top, sides and back of the spoon.

2 For clothes, cut a strip of felt the same length as the handle and wide enough to wrap around it. Glue and wrap the felt onto the spoon. Cut out and glue on felt accessories, such as bows, buttons, collars and belts.

3 Glue on googly eyes and add other features using marker pens.

You will need
(to make one puppet)
Wooden spoon
Acrylic paints and paintbrush
Pencil
Coloured permanent markers
Selection of felt scraps
Scissors
PVA glue
2 googly eyes

You can use double-sided tape instead of glue for quick and mess-free sticking.

87 Cardboard rocket

Transform old cardboard tubes and scraps of cardboard into this cool rocket. Kids will love decorating and personalizing it ready for a trip to the Moon. There's even a compartment for a little astronaut.

You will need

2 cardboard tubes, each about 5½in (14cm) long
Pencil, scissors and ruler
A4 sheet of silver and red card
A4 sheet of corrugated card
Masking tape
Red paint and paintbrush
Silver duct tape

A few small buttons
Strong glue
Tissue-paper scraps in red, orange and yellow
Pinking scissors (optional)
Plastic toy astronaut (or other type of figure) approx. 2½in (6cm) tall

1 Draw around the base of a tube onto red cardboard. Sketch a second circle, roughly ½in (1cm) bigger around the first one. Repeat, so that you have two circles. Cut out the circles and make little snips around the outside as far as the smaller circle. Fold them up into tabs.

2 Cut 2½in (6cm) off the end of one tube. Measure the height of the astronaut and cut a rectangle slightly taller than this from the larger tube. This will be the astronaut's compartment so it needs to be big enough for him to stand in.

3 Use masking tape to attach the tabbed circles inside the ends of the two tube pieces – they will go at either end of the astronaut's compartment, to ensure he or she doesn't slide up or down the rocket. Use masking tape to join together the tube pieces and the second tube.

4 For the rocket stand, draw three triangles onto corrugated card, each with two sides 3½in (9cm) long and the third 2½in (6cm) long. Use masking tape to attach them ½in (1cm) below the end of the tube base.

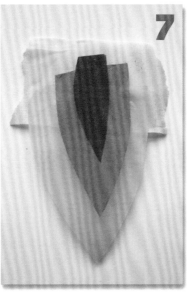

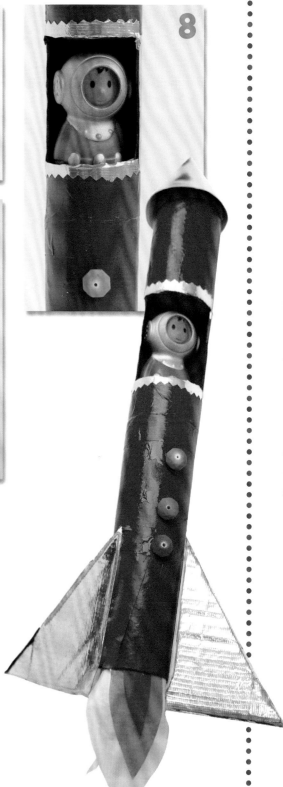

5 Paint the rocket red and leave it to dry. Glue buttons onto the rocket for decoration and cover the stand triangles using silver duct tape. Add a narrow strip of silver duct tape, trimmed with pinking scissors (if you have them), below the astronaut's window.

6 For the pointed top, draw and cut out a 4in (10cm) silver card circle. Cut away a third and overlap the cut edges to form a cone. Tape the edges together, then stick it to the top of the rocket using strong glue.

7 Cut yellow, orange and red tissue-paper flames and tape them inside the rocket base.

8 Pop in your astronaut and prepare for lift off!

88

Paper-plate tambourine

This sparkly tambourine is made with bells and filled with lentils so it isn't too noisy. You could also use different-sized plates and fill them with rice, or try using bottle tops for a different sound.

You will need
2 paper plates
Child-friendly paint and
   paintbrush
Glue stick and strong glue
2 handfuls of lentils or rice
Silver sequins
Single hole punch
4 silver bells
24in (60cm) ribbon

1 Paint the back of each plate with a few coats of paint and leave to dry. Glue on the sequins using the glue stick.

2 Pour the lentils or rice onto one of the plates and apply strong glue around the rim. Place the other plate on top and leave to set.

3 Use the single hole punch to make four evenly spaced holes around the rim of the plates. Cut the ribbon into four parts and thread each bell onto one. Feed the ribbons through the holes and secure with a knot.

89

Funny faces

This simple activity is guaranteed to raise giggles and requires few materials. You can cut out the facial features in advance and store them for a quick standby project. You could also cut out faces, bodies and clothes to make pictures of people wearing silly outfits.

Go through old magazines and cut out eyes, noses and mouths that are about 1in (2.5cm) or larger. Sort them into separate piles for ease – all the noses together, for example. Then draw a basic outline of a face and see who can make the craziest! Play around with different combinations before gluing down and embellishing with hair and accessories.

You will need
2–3 old magazines
Scissors
Glue stick
Paper
Colouring pens

Sock snowman

*This simple squashy snowman makes a cosy
winter friend to cuddle up with on a cold night.*

You will need
1 adult-sized white sock
Approx. 1½lb (600g) rice
Scissors and string
Strip of felt
2 small black buttons
1 orange button
Sewing needle and white thread
1 patterned baby sock

1 Turn the white sock inside out, pour in a third of the rice and twist the sock round tightly. Tie string around the twist to secure it and to make the head. Pour the remaining rice into the sock, twist and tie it with string as before to make the body.

2 Pull the open end of the sock up and over the body and head. You don't want lots of excess material so adjust it if necessary.

3 Cut a narrow strip of felt for a scarf and tie it around the neck. Sew on the buttons for the eyes and nose and slip the baby sock over the head for a cute little beanie hat.

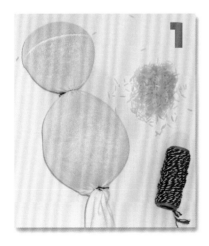

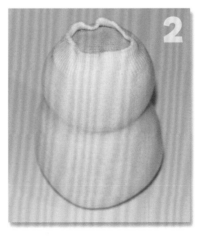

91

Felt owl

Making a soft toy is easier than you might think, so long as you keep the shapes nice and basic. Felt is a great first fabric for kids because it's cheap and easy to sew. You can sew an owl like this one or make any creature you like.

You will need
Tracing paper
Pencil
Scissors
Pins
2 A4 sheets of brown felt
Felt scraps in beige, black and red
Sewing machine (optional)
2–3 handfuls of toy stuffing
Sewing needle and thread

1 Photocopy the owl template (opposite), enlarging it by the amount shown. Remember that the main body piece will be sewn and turned out, so make it about ½in (1cm) bigger all the way round. Trace the individual parts of the owl onto tracing paper and then cut them out. Make sure you include 1½in (4cm) tabs for the wings and feet as shown on the template.

2 Pin the tracing-paper templates onto the felt and cut out the following: two body pieces and the wings from the brown felt, the outer eyes and feet from beige felt, the beak from red felt and the inner eyes from black felt.

You can sew your toy using a machine or by hand.

Owl template

Photocopy at 200%

3 Pin the outer eyes onto the body piece and sew them in place. Then pin and sew the black pupils on top. Pin and sew on the beak.

4 Pin the feet at the bottom of the body so that they face up and the wings at either side, facing in. Sew them in place.

5 Pin the two body pieces with right sides together. Sew around, about ½in (1cm) in from the edge, leaving a 2½in (6cm) gap at the head to allow you to turn out.

6 Turn the owl right sides out and stuff firmly.

7 Fold in the excess fabric at the gap, pin and hand stitch to join.

Dressing up

92 Pipe-cleaner crown

These crowns are a fantastic quick make when your little one decides it's time to be a king or a queen. Once you've built the basic crown you can embellish it – pompoms, sequins, cotton wool balls, gems and buttons all make nice additions.

You will need
About 15 pipe cleaners
A handful of pompoms
Double-sided sticky tape
   or strong glue
Scissors

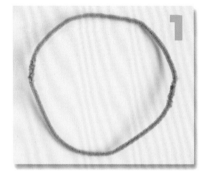

1 Join two pipe cleaners by twisting the ends together. Wrap this around the top of your child's head to make a hoop. Twist the free ends together.

2 To make the central heart, bend a pipe cleaner into shape and then wrap the ends around the hoop. Make sure the ends are concealed.

3 For the points, bend the remaining pipe cleaners into upside-down V shapes. Twist the ends to join them onto the hoop. Continue until you have filled up the whole hoop, then use scissors to snip off any excess pipe cleaner.

4 Attach a pompom to the tip of each point, using double-sided tape or strong glue.

For an extra-special touch use glittery pipe cleaners or thread pretty beads onto plain ones before attaching them to the basic hoop.

93 Paper-bead jewellery

Learn how to make simple and inexpensive beads from a sheet of paper. Kids will enjoy rolling up the paper and threading their own jewellery together.

You will need
Selection of A4 coloured
   paper
Pencil and ruler
Wooden skewers
Glue
Fine elastic
Needle with a large eye

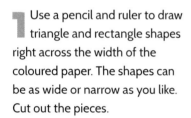

1 Use a pencil and ruler to draw triangle and rectangle shapes right across the width of the coloured paper. The shapes can be as wide or narrow as you like. Cut out the pieces.

2 To make the beads, spread glue on one side of a paper shape, leaving about 1in (2.5cm) unglued at the wider end. Place a skewer at this end and slowly roll up the paper around it. Remove the skewer and set the bead aside to dry for about an hour.

3 For a shiny finish, push several beads onto a skewer and paint them with a little more glue to varnish. Set the skewers across a pan or deep tray to let the beads dry.

4 Remove the beads from the skewers. Thread the elastic onto the needle and guide it through the beads, knotting it at both ends to secure.

Shrink-portrait key ring

A great last-minute activity, this takes no more prep than getting out the colouring pencils and the plastic shrinks satisfyingly in minutes. Just avoid water-based inks or pencils as they will leach colour once the plastic is baked.

You will need
Shrink plastic (1 A4 piece
    makes 4 key rings)
Colouring pencils
Permanent markers
Scissors
Hole punch
Metal key ring

1 Mark out a square roughly 6in x 6in (15cm x15cm) onto the shrink plastic sheet. This is the drawing area for your child's self-portrait. Colour the image as you would a normal picture.

2 Cut the picture out, leaving a border around the image to avoid sharp edges. Punch a hole at the top and bake, following the manufacturer's instructions.

3 Simply add a key ring and clip onto a pocket!

95 Magic-wand biscuits

These biscuits have simple ingredients and kids can be involved at every stage, from measuring out the ingredients and kneading the dough, to cutting the shapes and decorating.

 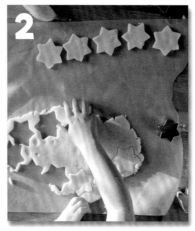 

You will need
(for approximately 12 biscuits)
3½oz (100g) chilled butter, cubed
3oz (85g) icing sugar
6oz (175g) plain flour
1 tsp vanilla extract
1 tbsp milk
1 egg yolk
Cling film
12 wooden skewers
2½in (7cm) star cookie cutter
Baking parchment

For the icing
14oz (400g) icing sugar
3–4 tbsp water
2–3 drops of 3 different food colourings
Cake toppings, such as gold sugar balls, butterflies, hundreds and thousands

1 Preheat the oven to Gas mark 4/180°C/350°F. Mix together the butter, sugar and flour. Rub together with your fingers until you have a breadcrumb-like texture. Mix in the egg yolk, vanilla extract and milk, then tip onto a work surface. Knead the mixture until you have a dough. Wrap the dough in cling film then place in the fridge for half an hour. Meanwhile, soak the skewers in water. Then roll out the dough on a floured surface to about ½in (1cm) thick.

2 Cut out star shapes using the cutter. Push a skewer into each star to resemble a magic wand. Place on a baking sheet lined with parchment paper and then bake for about 15 minutes in the centre of the oven, or until golden. Leave them to cool thoroughly.

3 Make the icing. Mix the icing sugar with water in a large bowl, a spoonful at a time, until it is runny but easy to spread. Separate into three smaller bowls and mix a little food colouring into each. Put a teaspoon into each bowl of icing and spread out the cake toppings within easy reach. Prepare for mess! The children can decorate their biscuits by spreading icing onto the wands before adding their favourite toppings.

Champion's medal

This medal is the perfect prize for mini-champs. This one is gold, but you can, of course, make a silver and bronze version to go with it.

1 Place the clay between two sheets of cling film – this will stop it sticking to your work surface and let you peel it away easily. Roll it out until it is about ¼in (5mm) thick.

2 Remove the top layer of cling film and use the cookie cutter to cut a circle from the clay. Use the pen lid to gently press circles onto the clay to make a pattern – be careful you don't press too deeply.

3 Line a baking tray with foil and bake your medal following the manufacturer's instructions. It should take about 30 minutes to cook. Once completely cooled, you can add a coat of varnish if you want an extra level of shine.

4 Glue the ribbon ends onto the back of the medal, ensuring the ribbon lays flat and there are no tangles.

You will need

1in (2.5cm) lump of yellow polymer clay
Cling film and rolling pin
30in (76cm) length of purple ribbon
2½in (6cm) circular cookie cutter
Craft varnish and paintbrush (optional)
Pen lid
Strong glue
Baking tray lined with foil

Polymer clay tends to be a little stronger but you could make it from air-dry clay and paint it gold.

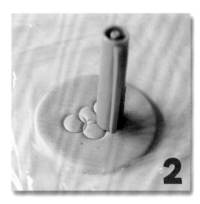

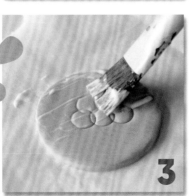

97 Felt superhero mask

Kids love dressing up and superheroes are equally popular with girls and boys. This mask is easy to sew on a machine or by hand. Younger children can sit on your knee and help you sew, while older children could sew by hand or have a go at the machine.

You will need

Mask template	Sewing thread and pins
A4 felt sheet	Fusible webbing
Scrap of felt in another colour	Iron
Scissors	Pencil
Sewing machine	16in (40cm) length thin elastic
Needle (optional)	

1 Photocopy and cut out the template below. Fold the A4 piece of felt in half and pin the template on top. Cut out two mask shapes. Using a scrap of felt, cut out a star shape and any other decorations you want.

2 Pin the star onto one of the mask pieces. If positioning around the eye, you will need to trim the star so that it doesn't overlap the hole.

3 Press the felt stars onto the mask piece using the fusible webbing and an iron, following the manufacturer's instructions. The iron must be used by an adult.

4 Stick the two mask pieces together using the webbing. Stitch around the mask, the eye-holes and the star as close to the edge as possible.

5 Transfer the two holes from the template onto the mask. Snip a tiny hole for each one. Thread the elastic through each end (using a needle if necessary) and secure with a knot on each side.

Mask template
Photocopy at 200%

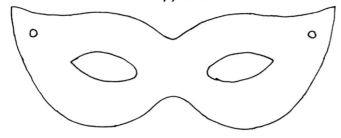

98

Pasta jewellery

This activity involves two stages – colouring the dried pasta and then threading it together. You can use any leftover pieces to create pretty pictures or to glue around a photo frame.

You will need
For the dye
3½oz (100g) uncooked pasta tubes, such as penne or macaroni
3½fl.oz (100ml) bottle sanitizing hand gel
Teaspoon
Food colouring in 4 contrasting colours
4 ziplock bags
4 toothpicks
Tray lined with baking parchment

For the jewellery
Beads
Thin elastic

1 Place two teaspoons of hand gel into a ziplock bag. Use a toothpick to add a small amount of food colouring. Close the bag and remove as much air as possible. Blend the liquids using your fingers until they are fully mixed. If you want a bright colour, add more food colouring to the bag.

2 Open the bag and add a quarter of the pasta. Reseal the bag and shake the pasta around until it is completely covered in the colour. Set the bag aside.

3 Repeat these steps to colour the rest of the pasta.

4 Gently tip each bag onto a different part of the lined tray, being careful not to let the colours touch. Leave them to dry overnight, then store in an airtight container.

5 Cut a length of elastic long enough for a necklace or a bracelet and tie a double knot 1in (2cm) from one end. Thread the pasta shapes mixed with beads onto the elastic.

6 Once full, tie a double knot at the other end of the elastic and then tie both ends together to finish.

Colourful pasta art

Different types of pasta can also be coloured and glued onto card to make pieces of art. Colourful penne pasta can be arranged to make a pretty rainbow, while yellow fusilli can be glued round a lion's face for a lovely big mane. Smaller pieces like macaroni can be arranged to make the petals on a flower, and bow-shaped pasta can be transformed into butterflies, hair bows or bow ties. You could also try embellishing a simple card frame with pasta and then painting it gold.

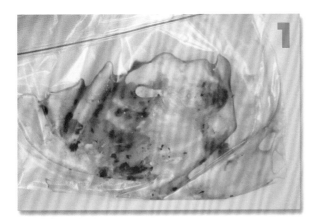

!

For added safety, you could use a quick-release magnetic clasp on your necklace.

Lion mask

This lovely lion is great for putting on a show. You don't have to make a lion though, you could make any animal you like. How about painting black and white stripes to create a zebra, or a pink pig mask with a snout cut from an egg carton?

You will need
Paper plate
Pencil
Hole punch
Yellow paint
Paintbrush
Small ball of yellow yarn
Double-sided sticky tape
Scraps of light-brown felt
Brown marker pen
16in (40cm) length of elastic

1. Draw eye shapes onto the back of the plate and cut out. Use an existing mask that fits to work out the dimensions, or measure the distance between your child's eyes using a tape measure.

2. Punch holes in the plate rim, one either side of the eyes and then paint the back of the plate yellow.

3. On the unpainted side of the plate, stick short strips of double-sided sticky tape around the edge, being careful not to tape over the punched holes. Wrap the yellow yarn in several layers around your fingers. Snip through the layers on either side to leave lots of individual strands, about 4in (10cm) long.

4. Press the yarn, several strands at a time, onto the double-sided tape. Go all the way round until you have created a thick woolly mane.

5. Cut out two ear shapes and a nose from the felt. Stick them on using double-sided tape.

6. Use the brown colouring pen to add the mouth, eyebrows and eyelashes. Finally, measure and cut the elastic to fit your child, feeding it through the holes and knotting to secure. Your king or queen of the safari is ready to go!

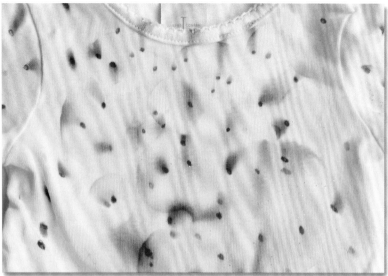

100 Tie-dye T-shirt

This is an easy way to create tie-dye effect clothing using permanent markers and rubbing alcohol (which is easy to find on the Internet).

!

The alcohol should be used only by an adult in a well-ventilated area, well away from children.

You will need
Plain white T-shirt
Permanent coloured markers
Rubbing alcohol
Pipette
Thick plastic bag
Iron

1 Lay the T-shirt out on a flat surface and place the folded plastic bag inside. This will stop any dye leaking through onto the back.

2 Get the child to doodle their design using the marker pens. Fill up as much of the T-shirt as you can with colour – the more you add, the more it will bleed and spread when the alcohol is added.

3 Now it's the adult's turn. Use the pipette to suck up the rubbing alcohol and squirt it over your design. Doing this several times – leaving to dry in between – will spread the colour further.

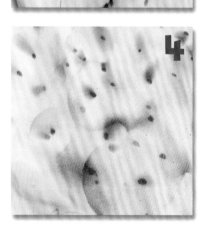

4 Once the T-shirt is completely dry, fix the colour by ironing it on a hot setting and then washing on a cool wash.

About us

Laura Minter and Tia Williams are crafters, mothers and writers. They started *Little Button Diaries*, their award-winning craft blog, to show that having children doesn't mean you have to stop doing the things you love. There is always time for crafting (as well as tea and biscuits)! They have written many craft books and created projects for major retailers Hobbycraft, Paperchase, Brother Sewing and Duck Tape. Between them, they have five children who they love to make things for (and with!).

Follow them at: littlebuttondiaries.com
Twitter: @LButtondiaries
Instagram: @littlebuttondiaries

Authors' acknowledgements

Thank you to everyone who has supported us while making this book – to our families whose houses we took over with our craft supplies, to our partners who got booted out for our many crafting days and to our friends who we tested all the craft successes and failures out on. Particular thanks to our Little Buttons, Amelie, Harper, Lilah and Grayson for being willing guinea pigs and for being involved with each and every one of these projects. We had a ball. X

Acknowledgements

All photos by Laura Minter and Tia Williams, except the following:

Page 8 (top-right): Shutterstock/Oksana Kuzmina

Page 10 (bottom-left): Shutterstock/ISchmidt

Page 11 (top-left): Emma Sekhon; (top-right): Shutterstock/Andrey_Kuzmin; (bottom-right): Shutterstock/wavebreakmedia

Page 12 (right): Emma Sekhon

Page 13 (top-right): Shutterstock/ Muskoka Stock Photos; (bottom-right): Shutterstock/Monkey Business Images

Pages 96 and 141: Emma Sekhon

Index

To place an order, contact:
GMC Publications Ltd
Castle Place, 166 High Street, Lewes,
East Sussex, BN7 1XU
United Kingdom
Tel: +44 (0)1273 488005
www.gmcbooks.com